Endo

"Rediscover Your Life After Loss is a must read guide for those who seek to discover some semblance of normalcy after experiencing life-altering grief and loss. Diann Pass offers real solutions and guidance as she shares her sacred journey of grief recovery and emotional healing. She 'keeps it real' in her personal account of caring for her husband from his diagnosis to his death, and everything in between. Pure essence of the reality every one of us will ultimately experience."

—Jacque Burklow, BSN RN, CHPCA,
Chief Operating Officer, Hospice of Midland

"Rediscover Your Life After Loss is a great resource for anyone who has lost a loved one, especially a spouse. No one better understands this kind of loss than someone who has lived it. Diann speaks from her heart and from experience. Her words will provide comfort, understanding, and guidance to those who are navigating the difficult road of grieving a spouse. Especially helpful are the Key Points and Moving Forward tips at the end of each chapter. This book would be a helpful guide for an individual to read and for grief support groups to work through together."

—Jan Reed, Pastor of Care Ministries at
St. Luke's United Methodist Church in Midland, Texas

"My good friend for many years, Diann Pass, eloquently brings to light one of the most difficult struggles we deal with in life in her new book, Rediscover Your Life After Loss. Have you lost someone close to you and aren't sure how to do life in this 'new normal'? Do you know someone who is struggling with the loss of a loved one?

Diann uses her firsthand knowledge of the journey from loss to recovery to illustrate for us how we can continue to choose life. She expands on her first book, Lessons in Living and Dying, and her vast experience as a chaplain to create the 'how to' document we all need. Don't wait until you need this great wisdom. Prepare for the inevitable battle of loss by arming yourself today. Adversity doesn't have to be so adverse. When we can understand the challenges that lie before us, it helps us better understand that there is a light at the end of the dark tunnel if we will keep moving forward. Let Diann help put to words what you will be going through and how to be an overcomer!"

—**David J. Kuhnert,** Production Manager,
CrownQuest Operating, author of Servant Leadership

"Diann Pass draws upon her personal journey of being a caregiver for her terminally ill husband to working through the stages of grief after his passing with such clarity and honesty. She comes alongside as a guide to show the way through what I call the pitfalls of grief. I would have greatly benefited from this book after the death of my son several years ago. I highly recommend it to anyone who is caring for a terminally ill loved one or walking through the valley of the shadow of death. It is truly a gift to us all—a beacon of hope to facilitate healing."

—**Emily Boller,** author of *Starved to Obesity*,
mother of five, artist and speaker

"My friend Diann Pass has done a superb job of covering all aspects of dealing with the loss of a loved one in this wonderful resource. Diann shares the advice that has been so instrumental in our family's emotional, spiritual and relational healing after we experienced the sudden death of our 22-month-old granddaughter. Her practical approach will be so beneficial to those going through the heartache of loss"

—Terri Dunn

"Diann has taken a subject most people do not want to talk about and dealt with it in raw and honest emotions. Some of it may not be the way you would tell your story or even believe, but that is the beauty of what she says: people approach and deal with grief in their unique way. Her style is easy to read and truly lets you look into her grieving mind – her journey. That is a big benefit of her book – candor about what she felt and did. Her honest and biting statements about things people say while around a grieving person provide insight, and she offers good tips on better things to say! Finally, her practical tips and lists are very useful."

—Hermann Eben, GR8 Solutions Group

"Diann Pass provides a bridge to close the gap between the pain of a loved one's death and the healing process of those left behind. Readers' hearts are strengthened as Diann shares her real-life experience after walking through the shadows of death."

—Roy Smith, Senior Pastor and Founder,
True Lite Church, Midland, Texas

"This book is filled with encouragement and reassurance that grief is a season, a purpose as defined in God's word. The author walks with you through your stages of grief, promising that one day you will be able to face your future, and offers ideas on how to accomplish that new direction. She speaks from experience. As our chaplain, she did this for me beginning the day my daughter-in-law was diagnosed with breast cancer until we lost her five years later. She prayed with me, cried with me, offered scriptures to ease the ache, and celebrated when we received a piece of good news. I think you will be comforted and inspired when you read this book."

—**Cecile Wiginton,** CP, Paralegal,
Arrington Oil & Gas Operating, LLC

REDISCOVER YOUR LIFE AFTER LOSS

REDISCOVER YOUR LIFE AFTER LOSS

DIANN PASS

ISBN: 978-1-7339960-2-0 (paperback)
ISBN: 978-1-7339960-0-6 (hardback)
ISBN: 978-1-733-9960-1-3 (ebook)

All Scripture quotations, unless otherwise indicated, are taken from the Holy Bible, New King James Version R Copyright ©1982 by Thomas Nelson. Used by permission. All rights reserved.

Unless otherwise noted, the stories in this book are based on a collection of client experiences. Names and identifying information have been changed to protect the person's privacy.

Disclaimer: The information in this book is designed to provide helpful information on the subjects discussed based on the author's opinions. It is not intended to be a substitute for legal or financial advice for your specific situation.

Cover and Interior Design: Jerry Dorris, AuthorSupport.com

First printing April 2019/ Printed in the United States of America

*This book is dedicated to those living in grief
after the death of someone they love.
May you find strength and hope for your journey
and may the joy of life be your reward.*

Contents

GUIDE TO
CAREGIVING

Introduction

If you are reading this, more than likely you have lost a spouse or someone you love deeply, or perhaps you're trying to help someone you know who has lost a loved one. There is nothing that compares to the loss of a spouse. There is not even a synonym for the word *widow*. Look in the thesaurus and you will find that I am correct. I don't want to compare the loss of a spouse to other losses; the death of anyone you love is shocking and horrible. But there is something strikingly dreadful about losing the one you woke up next to day after day. Your best friend. Your lover. Your confidant. Your solace through the worst times. Someone who shared the jokes known only by the two of you. Two becoming one. Most of us worked hard to achieve the unity that marriage brings. Suddenly, it's jerked away! Solo. Single. Solitary.

I have walked through grief both as a chaplain of more than a decade and personally with the death of my husband. During my own journey, I read more than twenty-five books. I'm certain I would not have read so many except something was missing that propelled me to pick up yet another book and then another. Most books offer lots of information about the interminable devastation of grief, but I needed more than that. I needed practical information too, to get through each moment, each day. Along with that, I wanted to develop a healthy mindset, not that of a victim. I wanted direction in developing life after such horrific loss.

I set out to write a book that would acknowledge the beginning and its difficulties; specific challenges along the journey; and finally, what dreaming a new dream would look like.

This book contains remembrances from my life with my wonderful husband along with practical information that I have learned—both as a chaplain and through the personal experience of losing my own husband. There are many concrete things that you need to know when you lose a beloved spouse. I hope that this book reveals a few of those to you. I also hope that the sweet stories of times with my own husband will help you to relive precious moments from your own marriage. If the loved one you lost is not a spouse or partner, be aware that even though my loss was a spouse, there are many experiences that you will go through that are common to loss.

If you are on this same journey, I will share helpful information with you that I had to ferret out for myself. Grief should only be a season of your life. It should not last forever. Grief is a journey, not a destination. The goal is to survive the pain and use it to make the next season of your life richer—and to extend a hand to others who will inevitably walk this path in due time.

I hope you find healing, courage, and vision within these pages.

My Story

Are you like most people and have a really hard time with the idea of death? Thinking about it. Being around it. Talking to those in grief. Can you say the word *death*? Very few people use the words *death*, *dying*, or *died*. There are so many euphemisms for the word *death*: *in a better place*, *six feet under*, *cashed in*, *checked out*, *kicked the bucket*, *pushing up daisies*. Then, some of my personal favorites *bought the farm*, *taking a dirt nap*, and for you cowboy types, *last round-up*. Unfortunately, my last name is one of the most commonly used euphemisms for death—*pass* or *passed*. When my husband died a few years ago, I was amused by those who inquired if he had "passed." My reply to one person was:

"What else would he do?" They were horrified rather than amused!

Death. A part of life. Not the good part, but definitely a part. When death is staring you in the face, as it was me in 2010, you must decide whether to deny it or embrace it. Lots of people choose to ignore the obvious, and in a very Pollyanna manner, act as if dying is not a possibility. It has been my experience that the dying desire, even *need*, to talk about death. It's the people around them who have the difficulty.

When my husband was facing death, he boldly announced one day that he prayed at night not to wake the next day. I considered the implications before I responded. After having been a chaplain for several years, I knew I should encourage him to talk about death rather than shutting him down. I told him that I thought I could understand—because of how terrible he felt and the hopelessness of his disease. I told him it was hard for me to hear, but I understood.

We sat there that day, in our rocking chairs, overlooking the golf course. The golfers were very much alive on the other side of the fence—laughing, cursing their bad shots, drinking beer. On our side of the fence, we quietly reflected on the end of a brilliant life. We sat and he talked about his death. His fear. His anticipation. Things I would need to know when he was gone. After about twenty minutes, we both became quiet, lost in our own thoughts. Finally, I said to him, "Want me to get the pillow?" He laughed and said, "No. Not yet."

Over the next two years, the door swung open wide to numerous conversations about death. He gave me priceless advice for the future —who to talk to about different investments, the house, the car, filing the taxes, and more. His wisdom that I had relied upon for three decades.

I look back on that day and see what a momentous time it was—a time when we both began to process our individual futures. For him, death and eternity. For me, an eternity of alone. I treasure that day because we began to walk the path in a very intimate way. You see, nothing can be more intimate than sharing tender talks about a life that is ending, a future that will never be. Dreams now dying too. On that day, we went from picking our way carefully through sticky predictable conversations—How are you feeling today? Did you sleep? What are you hungry for? We then placed our feet squarely into never-before spoken chasms of fear.

Facing fear reduces the challenge from insurmountable to a hill that's climbable. I didn't say *want* to climb, but a hill that must be climbed! I had no idea of the heartbreak that was rushing at me. There's no way to anticipate the loss of *presence* of a loved one. After John's death on 12-12-12, I grieved. I cried daily for eight months. I cried when I got up in the morning and saw the single coffee cup. I cried when the mail came and I was no longer Mrs. John Pass, but Ms. Diann Pass. I cried at church because I was there alone. Everything changed. Sleeping alone. Eating alone. No one touched me anymore. I missed touch the most. I still do! Life as I knew it was gone—forever. In fact, as happens with lots of widows, I felt like my life was over, even though I was still breathing.

I decided to be the best I could be with what remained of my life—to be a good mother, grandmother, chaplain, Christian, friend. Even though my life was now a monotone of sadness.

The five stages of grief: overwhelming grief, daily grief, crushing grief, staggering grief, paralyzing grief. Those are not exactly the five stages of grief you've read about, but trust me, they are the real stages. They are accompanied by: Who's going to take out the trash now? When do I buy new tires? How do I make the commode stop making that noise? And *what* was that sound I heard in the night?

These are the thoughts and a short synopsis of the feelings and challenges of those early days. Raw. No other word sufficiently defines those first twelve months for any of us experiencing loss of a loved one.

Unfortunately, the second and third years after loss can continue to be a downhill slide. That first year, we grieve the loss of the person. In the time to come, we grieve the loss of the relationship, the companionship, the new loneliness.

That was the overview. Now back to the very beginning. We didn't know it was the beginning. We thought it was a doctor's appointment to diagnose shortness of breath that had been progressing slowly. John had bypass surgery the year before and had excellent progress since but had begun this shortness of breath in the last few months. We were both hoping for a pill or some physical therapy. Something simple.

Besides, the day was beautiful, and we were looking forward to lunch with our daughter and dinner with friends. We had married in 1984 while living in Dallas and it was always a treat to be there. Always nostalgic. When we would leave to return home, we called it leaving home to go home. Family, friends, fun places with loving memories.

Here we were waiting to see the pulmonologist. I looked over at John. After all these years, the nearly thirty since I first met him, he still looked the same to me. His hazel eyes had a sparkle and a warmth that enveloped you and pulled you into his world. I loved being a part of his world and even though I know time had changed him I could not see it. John's black hair had been painted along the sides with gray even then. Being honest, it was grayer now. He still didn't look old to me. He looked up and smiled that all encompassing smile that said I was the only person in the room. I smiled back. Thinner. Definitely thinner. He still had that Clark Gable movie star quality. Ruggedly handsome. I looked back at my magazine and smiled to myself, lost for a moment in my good fortune of having snagged the best-looking guy in the room. The waiting room.

The cardiologist had referred us to this pulmon- ologist, and we were not at all anxious as we sat there waiting. We had lots of plans for the next decade of our life and we were excited to begin. It felt as if we could begin those plans as soon as we checked off this doctor's appointment. Plans for retirement and a new retirement home in the Big Bend area of Texas. Plans to travel more. Plans for more time together. I didn't realize then that this was one too many "ologists" in our phone book!

Imposing was the only word I had for the doctor. All the staff seemed a little afraid or awed of the man. I still can't be certain which. He was a large man, tall and not at all thin. His head was bald on top and very wiry gray around the sides and back. I thought he looked like a character out of the Old Testament, maybe Noah or Moses. He was all business. His voice was gruff as he shook our hands and sat down on a small rotating stool before a computer. Dr. Jones turned to consult the computer. Apparently, the questionnaire John had completed was now entered into the computer along with John's previous records from the open-heart surgery. Dr. Jones began to ask John questions. At some point John turned to me for an answer. When I did answer, Dr. Jones glared at me. I made a note to myself not to answer any more questions!

The verdict came out of the blue and was not at all what we were expecting. "You are in the beginning stages of emphysema, Mr. Pass." Wow! I was floored, but I guess it would not be fair to say surprised. John had smoked for decades even though he had given up the habit ten years earlier. The balance of what Dr. Jones said to us that day made me feel as if I was in a tunnel and the sound was echoing off its sides. Listening as carefully as I could, I let John ask all the questions. After all, it was his health.

In the end, there was only one medication pre-scribed, and it was only to slow the disease, not cure it. The only cure is a lung transplant and they are not done for anyone over sixty. John attempted to plead his case for how young he felt and how great his health was. Dr. Jones looked at him and repeated, "Sixty." The other thing was oxygen. John would require oxygen at night. Seems that oxygen rates drop at night. I don't think I ever asked why. Sleeping? Laying down?

I don't remember much about the rest of our day. Someone asked about his doctor's appointment. John replied that he had a little emphysema. I guess that was a true description, though maybe *early* emphysema was more accurate. A *little* emphysema was like a being a little pregnant. Life changing!

Neither of us had any idea what we were facing. Dr. Jones had said that John would have several more years of life, and further, that he would probably not die from emphysema. It seems something like a common cold can turn into pneumonia and end up taking your life rather than the emphysema itself. A *little emphysema* indeed.

As we drove the five hours back to West Texas, we discussed the retirement home we were building. Fortunately, we had not yet begun building. We had been working on house plans. Had secured the land but not closed on it. We were working on a water well, electricity, and clearing the carefully chosen site.

We had spent many hours on that site, sitting in a vehicle in the late afternoon watching the wild game graze—the deer, the aoudad sheep, birds, and even a bear. It was fascinating to sit there quietly and watch the game and dream of sitting on our own front porch someday after the house was built.

The decision was painful, but we both knew it was the right decision. We should not build the house. There was no hospital near there and John could need emergency medical care periodically. We were devastated. I didn't understand then what I see so clearly now in the rearview mirror. This was the beginning of the end. The beginning of loss. It was huge. The death of a dream. Not a small loss. We both grieved. I watched as John rolled up the architectural plans and put them in the back of his closet, where I rediscovered them a year ago.

We called and the oxygen was delivered, like milk or the morning paper. Brought right into our home. The darn oxygen concentrator weighed thirty-five pounds and made a terrible noise. Not a horrible noise like an MRI but a distracting noise made into the dead of night, almost like breathing except exponentially louder. In the beginning I would lay awake and listen to the sound. A sound that represented life to John and death to me.

Neither of us had faced a serious illness before. We didn't know what to expect and I was quite surprised when people said thoughtless things. "You didn't need another home to take care of." "God didn't want you to spend time away from church." (How did they know what God wanted?) "Don't worry about the oxygen; I see people walking in the mall with it all the time!" John's reply was, "But it is not you!" A foreshadowing of the thoughtless things people would say after he died. Well-meant, but thoughtless at the same time.

In many ways the disease was slow-moving, but in many ways not. Immediately, John quit carrying anything because it added to his lack of breath. We had always been partners in everything. John took out the trash and made the bed. He could do neither without being winded. And, when we packed the car, including the new oxygen tanks, I had to pack it. I would sleep for the first thirty minutes of any road trip, exhausted from packing the so-called portable oxygen equipment. We could no longer fly. The process of flying with oxygen was complicated and frightening. Plus, he could no longer be at altitudes over five thousand feet without oxygen. This meant that we were stuck in the desert in the heat of the summer.

Don't misunderstand. I would trade all the cool temperature of the past six years for one more week in the hot summer if I could have him back. It doesn't work that way! The changes, even in the beginning, were dramatic. The grieving doesn't wait for death. It begins with the loss of dreams, of independence, literally of your future. Our world got smaller and smaller as the disease progressed and John became more fragile. Then one day, we both got a new life. For him, eternity. For me, an eternity of alone. And that's when I began to have a fuller understanding of grief.

I wanted to tell you my story first. Along the way you will see the many facets of grief. You too will find that telling and retelling your story is part of your healing, part of acceptance. If you are on this same journey, you will find that sometimes the path is level. But often, it is steep and rocky, and we stumble and fall back. One of my goals is to help you learn to anticipate, interpret, and finally accept some of the surprises and challenges that await you.

The Color
of Grief

I returned to church, to work, and to most activities immediately after Christmas, which was just over two weeks after the loss of my husband. Back to Bible study. Because of my husband's illness, these were things I had not done for more than a year. People began to tell me how great I looked! I didn't understand—were they trying to make me feel better?

I realized that I experienced times when I felt almost euphoric. What was that? A friend who was a counselor told me that for the first time in a very long time, I was participating in life. I was no longer confined to my home. I had color in my cheeks. I was breathing life instead of death. But, oh my, when I would fully comprehend the reason for my euphoria, I would crash. I've never taken drugs, but I could imagine that the crash I was feeling was not unlike coming down off a drug high. Death had removed my constraints—the jail that had confined me. The crash always happened at home. No one else was subjected to it, but it was a doozy. I didn't really want to feel good about something that was so terrible. So very confusing. So very common.

Common. I like the word *common*. My pastor liked the word *normal*, but I have great objection to it. For me, the word *normal* felt exclusive, like a club to join, or maybe even a judgment. At a time of so much pain, I did not need to feel further excluded! Everyone will experience these grief moments at a different pace. Everyone has different circumstances. Everyone has a different relationship. Everyone has different things left unresolved. So, the word I use is *common*.

What is happening to you is common to what you are going through. We are all going to experience some or most of the stages of grief that Elisabeth Kubler-Ross wrote of—denial, anger, bargaining, depression, and acceptance. We are going to experience them at different rates, and at different times, and perhaps, some not at all. What does that mean? Nothing. We are all individuals. The number of tears that fall or the length of time they come does not mean anything. If you don't cry for eight months, yay for you! If you cry for twelve, does that mean you loved your mate more than I loved mine? No. No. No. There is no barometer that measures pain. If you had fewer tears, maybe you are healthier, or perhaps you had better coping skills, or perhaps you are suppressing those emotions that are so very painful to express. If you had more tears, perhaps you had more things left unresolved!

No one who has had a loss will urge you to get on with your life or get over it. Those who have never experienced loss fail to understand that grief takes as long as it takes. Some wise person did tell me to cry the tears whenever they came. Don't put them off. When you do that, you will pass up the opportunity to cry them at all. You will cry them at some point, but the more you suppress them, the harder it is to cry them, and the more likelihood that you will cry them at some inopportune time in the future. Who wants to be sitting with friends at some lovely dinner three or four years later and break into big, ugly sobs! Cry them now when they are expected! I compare those times to deferred interest. No one likes to pay interest, but when we buy something with the idea of deferring the interest until later, we must be careful not to violate the terms of the agreement. Deferred interest may work well for purchasing an appliance but deferring grief until later doesn't work well for the one grieving Do it now! You will also have times nearing the euphoria that I spoke of earlier—unexplained times of bliss. Don't feel guilty when those times come. They will pass quickly. Grab every moment of relief that comes your way. You will need those moments to carry you through the times of despair that will flood your soul as you walk through this period of grief. Remember the good and precious times. Don't focus on the fact that they will never come again but focus on gratitude that you had them at all!

Some people walk through this life without a good marriage or a good partner. If you have had one, be grateful. Gratitude is healing. Even in your grief, your darkness will be lifted if you can experience gratitude for the good that you were blessed with. Don't peer at your future and think what might have been. Try hard—I know it's difficult—to be thankful for what was!

If you did not have a good marriage, you must still heal. Some of what you are grieving will be that lack of time to repair your marriage. That cannot be changed now.

Forego all guilt if you can. Guilt is an emotion that holds no healing for you. Guilt is an emotion that drags you down and throws you into second guessing. Unfortunately, second guessing is not helpful—not in any way. It is easy to look back and wish that some things said or done could have been changed. If you need to, address it early on with a friend or counselor, but don't set up housekeeping there. The facts cannot be changed now. Things are now set in stone. A headstone, if you will.

For people who spend inordinate amounts of time looking back, wishing things could have been different or words could be unsaid, it is best to put those thoughts out of your mind. Scripture calls it taking every thought captive.

Different people have different ways of achieving that captivity of their thoughts. For me, I try to find a scripture that is short and pertains to the fight I am engaged in. Then, every time I have a negative thought pertaining to that thought pattern, I say the verse—out loud. It is a sort of reprogramming.

There are other methods that I am certain would also be helpful. One could think back to another happier time in the relationship. Refocus. In whatever way you achieve the reprogramming or the refocus, it is necessary to press on to a place where you allow yourself peace in the circumstances as they occur. They cannot be changed! Don't spend time there! Elisabeth Kubler-Ross said, "Death has a cruel way of giving regrets more attention than they deserve." You have grieving to do! It is your full-time job until you are in a more stable place—a place of acceptance where you are no longer second-guessing things that cannot be changed.

Grieving is your full-time job now. That's depressing, isn't it? Not really. You need to give yourself permission to stay in this place until you have completed your work here. Grief is a natural response to the loss of someone whom you loved. Grief is an emotional response, but it usually impacts us socially, physically, and culturally as well.

In fact, one of the most difficult challenges of death is the cultural change. I live in a relatively small city. If there are singles groups, I have yet to find them. I was married. I was part of a couple. Now, I am single. Our couple friends no longer feel comfortable inviting me to "couple events." The result is that people I love no longer spend time with me. We, as widows/widowers, must now do two things: The first is to realize that our friends still love us. They feel awkward. They fear that we will feel uncomfortable in a group of couples. Truth is, we will feel that discomfort, but it is incumbent upon us to work through those feelings. We must either forego those friends by spending less time with them or accept our current circumstances. The second thing we must do is cultivate opportunities to invite those friends to participate in our life—much as we would have if our spouse was still alive. We can still invite friends to dinner. We can still purchase tickets to the symphony or the basketball game. We must let our friends know that we desire to continue to be a part of their lives!

Grief is, in fact, all-encompassing. Sadly, if grief had a color, it would be gray. A color devoid of light. Not hopeless, not black, but gray, the winter of one's life. The time before spring that heralds new life.

Sue and Brad's Story

One day in November 2011, I was making my regular chaplain rounds at one of the companies where I worked. The receptionist asked if I would speak to a young man who was pacing in the lobby. She told me that his wife was in the hospital with a potentially fatal condition. Brad was forty-two years old. His wife, Sue, had contracted an autoimmune condition of her lungs that had come on quite suddenly and only a few weeks later was threatening her life. Weeks passed in the hospital—one day she was given a five percent chance to live. Her sweet husband wanted to take her home. I urged him not to do that since someone has to be among that five percent. And, thankfully, she was part of that five percent!

Day after day, night after night. Sue would climb the mountain and then slide back down, looking death in the face again. Hope regained and then quickly dashed once again. Lungs are still challenging to the medical community. Transplants offer the most hope, especially for the autoimmune condition Sue had contracted.

Weeks turned into months. After four months, Sue left the hospital and was able to attend the college graduation of their oldest daughter. I'm certain the entire family experienced incredible hope for a new beginning. Unfortunately, that roller coaster went on for two more years of hospitalization, with brief intervals at home.

Sue spoke with lung experts who said her only real hope was a lung transplant. Sue and Brad made the three hundred-mile trip to see the team. Tests were done. Tissue matching, blood tests, and oxygen tests were done to identify the process of finding matching lungs.

A plan. Now, there was a plan. A plan for health. A plan for life. A plan for a future. Those hopes were dashed again when the blood-matching test identified a blood condition that made the likelihood of a match nearly impossible.

Sue was one of the most delightful people I have ever met. Charming. Energetic. She was a beautiful woman whose entire body seemed to smile. She exuded friendliness. And fun. She and I had an instant connection—once I was finally able to meet her. I never visited until she went home. She was way too sick for anyone but family in the hospital. So, during those hospital days, I camped out with her family in cold, harsh waiting rooms. I got to know her through her mother and father, daughters, brother, in-laws. Many hours spent in the lonely, sterile halls of healing. There were tears and laughter, both a part of life.

The next couple of years went by with little or no change. Trips to see the transplant team. Oxygen being increased. The tether that brings life—life and prison. The prison of promised health, but never reaching anything near freedom from the ball and chain known as the oxygen machine.

Fragile was the only constant in the life of Sue and Brad, but they found it great to be home, together again. They were spending time with family and friends. Going to church. The oldest daughter got married. Great mile markers. Then, the ultimate for most parents, a grandchild.

A few months after the birth came the holidays and the flu. After only a few days in the hospital on January 2, 2016, Sue took her last breath. And on a gray January day she rose to her well-earned place with the other saints, free at last of the oxygen machine that had tethered her to this world.

Key Points

1. Grief is all-encompassing.
2. Grief is a natural response to the loss of someone you loved.
3. Grief is different for each person but can have many things in common.

Moving Forward

Lean into your grief. Don't run from it or shy away from tears. Spend as much time alone as you need grieving and also as much time as you need with others. Your job now is to grieve. Be in denial, be angry, negotiate with God. All these will help you to walk through your grief.

*   *   *

UPDATE: Prior to publishing I gave "Brad" an opportunity to read the story about he and his wife, "Sue." He approved the copy, but also said that my readers deserved an update on Brad after Sue. Here is that update in his own words. "Your words brought back so many memories from those painful and joyful years. Sue helped us so much in those five years because of her faith and teachings which helped us all to move forward with life. I had so many GRAY days and still do, but I am beginning to see colors again, and for that I am grateful and know that there is a future for me. The day to day struggle of not being able to BREAKDOWN (great song by Cross Canadian Ragweed). I had to take care of others that were hurting and try to keep things in line and it never allowed me to breakdown or grieve for nearly a year. On February 16, 2017, I finally hit a wall, and I totally smashed into it. That was the best thing that could have happened, because then I was able to get on with life. God allowed me time to Breakdown, and He built me back up. I will forever cherish the twenty-four years I had with "Sue", but now I also realize there are great times ahead for me."

Help!
I'm Losing
My Mind

O ne of the most monumental problems that I think most widows/widowers encounter, and in fact, almost anyone who faces grief after loss, is that grief makes you truly feel as if you are losing your mind. Simply said, grief is overwhelming. You're unable to focus or read or watch TV. You are not able to choose a selection from a menu.

When you feel these thoughts and sensations, do not lose hope. There are steps you can take to navigate through your life. First, make as few decisions as possible. Then, make some guidelines for yourself that will aid in making decisions. I learned that I had trouble deciding on food choices from the menu, even from places I had frequented for years. I would ask my dinner partner what they were having, then I too would select that item. Bingo! Decision made! And the anxiety of decision-making would disappear. Also, make lists. Then set alarms on your phone that remind you to check those lists. Have close friends or family members call and remind you of engagements and deadlines. Don't rely on your brain, which is overwhelmed and is attempting to process all the change.

One story that still haunts me is that of some friends who lost their grandchild in a tragic circumstance. As I sat with them the following day, I related this information to them: Grief is overwhelming, and you will feel as if you are losing your mind. Time passed and I watched their journey through the darkest time. One day the husband, a successful businessman, told me how he had thought that he would be exempt from the confusion of grief. After all, he reasoned, he was involved in business, in public affairs, and had a large and busy family. He told of working an entire week with most of his organization preparing for a presentation to a large group of investors. On Monday morning he got up, packed a bag, and headed for the airport. When almost there, he remembered the large contingent of investors who were at his office! He conceded the point. Grief is overwhelming and makes it extremely challenging to focus. You will not lose your mind, but you will *feel* like that is the case.

You see, our minds are programmed for a daily regimen that no longer exists. Our days revolved around schedules of when he/she came home from work, left for work, etc. After the loved one's death, our brain is trying to determine exactly what to do with those pre-programmed events.

The answer is to make a new routine. Make changes to be busy during the most challenging times of the day. Such changes are not unlike being on a diet and changing our habits at the time of day that we are most tempted to snack. A change of habit doesn't totally solve the problem, but it helps!

There is no hurry. Change takes time. Grieve. Don't rush. Grief is a slow process. Give yourself grace. Lean into the pain. Accept that these feelings are only for a time. Walk through the grief as slowly as need be. Acknowledge the pain of loss. Denial is such a strong emotion, but denial is not necessarily an unhealthy emotion. In the beginning denial allows your mind time to adjust and confront the loss. As time goes on denial is much easier than doing the work that healing requires.

A friend who loves me dearly said one day that she thought I was depressed. I was wholly offended! I replied that I was not depressed. I was in grief! I didn't have some chemical imbalance in my brain!

My sadness was real and deep, and like a deep physical wound, it needed to heal. A wound that needed attention like a physical wound requires attention. This wound needed a bandage sometimes, and sometimes it needed fresh air. Sometimes a wound requires ointment to assist in healing—time with friends who loved me and patiently listened to my stories from the life that no longer existed!

Women do interesting things—we sleep in the T-shirts our husbands once wore. We make new stuff out of his old stuff. We join a group to extinguish whatever took the life of our loved one. (Mothers Against Drunk Driving is one good example.) A friend sprayed a shirt lightly with his favorite cologne and slept next to it every night for a while. I did many things to memorialize my husband's life. I made necklaces from the coin cufflinks I had given him as a wedding gift. I made a necklace from the gold piece he carried as a money clip. I had quilts made from his shirts. I wrote and published a book, *Lessons in Living and Dying*, a collection of essays honoring his life. I held tightly to everything that had belonged to him. But it was just stuff. Comforting stuff for a while, but just stuff.

I clung to my faith, and ultimately it was my faith that got me to the other side. I went back to church immediately. I cried through every service. Mostly, I sat alone. I felt alone. I wore my grief like an amulet.

I was not in denial. I just wanted to sit alone. I hated alone, but at church I wanted to sit alone with my grief. There was comfort in being able to express my grief there without being judged. These people had loved him too. So, there I would be on Sunday morning, with tears washing down my face in sheets. It was a quiet cry—not disturbing to others—but the tears would wash away my makeup and leave me fresh of face—if not spirit!

I began each new week with a verse from scripture that would comfort me. The first verse I chose was John 1:16, which says, "And from His fullness we have all received grace upon grace." I can no longer be certain what prompted me to choose that verse from the many comforting verses in scripture, but even though I was hurting deeply, I felt gratitude for the many wonderful years I had shared with my husband. I pursued a path—even in the very beginning—that rejected bitterness and chose to recognize that death is a real part of life. I still say, "It's not the good part, but it is definitely a part. No one gets out alive or unscathed!"

We have all heard this bit of wisdom: Do not make any major life decisions for the first year. It is common to want to move soon after a death. The reason we should not do that is this confusion we are dealing with. I fully understand the desire to get away from the stifling pain. The problem is that the pain is within our hearts and we cannot get away from it by moving! Because of our inability to make a good decision, anything sounds better than living alone in grief. Nothing could be further from the truth! We can make bad decisions that last for years. Investments, new homes, or new relationships can all have long-lasting consequences. Better to wait until our minds are clear.

One friend was discussing moving his mother into a smaller home, nearer to him. She totally bought into the idea. He asked me what I thought. Boldly, I told him that of course she wants to move. She has lived in that house for decades with her husband. As she looks around her, she remembers the story of every item that was purchased, its initial cost. Was it a gift? If so, for what occasion? Those memories can bring joy, but initially they tend to bring anguish. The anguish of loss.

The point to these reflections is that grief brings confusion, befuddlement, and a long-lasting fog. Grief takes time and is a slow walk, not a sprint. Hebrews 12:2 says "let us lay aside every weight and the sin that so easily ensnares us and let us run with endurance the race that is set before us." Grief will be a part of that race for every human being. We are asked to lay aside not only our sin but the distractions that take us away from the race. Death is not a distraction. Grief is a natural part of life. But we cannot tarry unreasonably in a season of grief. No one can tell you how long that season is for you, but do not set up camp there.

There is healing, but not before you face the high hurdles. You cannot go around the troubles of life. You must go through them. Problems not faced may be hidden for a time, but the pain and angst will return, and usually with a vengeance. Face the unknown with courage. Someone once said that we can trust our unknown future to a known God. I like that. If you are a person of faith, don't begin to doubt your faith when things are challenging. This is the time to prove your faith. They call it faith for a reason. Belief in what you cannot see. Belief that not only will you survive, but you will thrive again!

And, do not be chagrined if you decide to seek counseling. Some of us have friends who listen and are helpful. Others of us are more private and do not want to discuss these most intimate feelings with our friends. We find safety in anonymity!

Mary Jane's Story

Mary Jane and her husband, Stan, lived a quiet life in East Texas. Stan was a physician of some renown in the area and had done quite well for himself financially. Mary Jane and Stan were in the process of building a large compound down on the Texas coast—large enough for all the family, but it could also be rented when they weren't there. The added income meant that the compound would be self-sufficient and pay for itself in the long-term. They were almost giddy as their dream reached fruition.

Then, Stan was killed in an auto accident. Mary Jane was left with the compound. It was too large for her to want to manage alone. Within a year, she sold the compound. And, within the year, she was being squired around by a younger man. The attention was wonderful! Mary Jane felt alive again, desirable. Her steel blue eyes danced as she spoke of her new relationship and they married quickly. Quickly, she began to see large sums of money disappear from her checking account. Mary Jane watched it carefully, knowing all too well it was the newer, younger man she had brought into her life. For months Mary Jane avoided broaching the subject with him. But the time came when she could no longer ignore what was plain to see. First, she told her daughters that she had made a huge mistake. They agreed because they could see the large amounts of money being spent by the new husband. Mary Jane got a divorce before Stan had been dead two years!

I think Mary Jane is a perfect example of why we should not make decisions—especially such huge decisions—too soon. The consequences of her impulsive decision were a messy, expensive divorce.

And, more than that, she experienced shame over her quick decision to remarry.

> ### *Key Points:*
>
> 1. Grief is overwhelming.
> 2. Make as few life-changing decisions as possible.
> 3. Get counseling if need be.

Moving Forward

Recognize that the feelings of confusion and your lack of ability to focus are common to grief!

Negotiating with God

There is no way to prepare for the loss of your partner. No amount of time can prepare one for the finality—the loss of presence. My husband, John, was ill for seven years. At the beginning, his illness was more of a hindrance than anything else. Emphysema begins slowly. Each day is a degeneration. Each day needs to be celebrated because tomorrow will not be as good as today. I'm certain many other diseases are not unlike that.

First, John suffered from shortness of breath. Every little activity made him short of breath, so I tried to perform those tasks that made him winded. Take out the trash. Those kinds of tasks. In the beginning he used oxygen only at night while he slept. I found it almost impossible to sleep with that oxygen machine assaulting my ears all night. I found my own breathing tied rhythmically to the sound. I had no idea at that time how much I would hate the sound of it twenty-four hours a day, and even more shocking, how quiet my life was when it was gone. How I missed that sound. The sound of life! I was now assaulted by the silence just as I had been by the noise. How confusing!

Things disappeared slowly from our lives. Flying became such a challenge and going to any place with altitude was out because oxygen was even more challenging in altitude. The result was that all the cool places we had once escaped to in August were forbidden—Colorado, Santa Fe, Ft. Davis, Mt. Kilimanjaro (just kidding). So, in August while our friends left our very hot desert homes, we sweated it out—literally. Stuck. Sentenced to summers in the heat. For the last few years of his life, we would drive to Dallas (to see a child and the doctor) or to Austin (to see another child). Other than that, we were confined in our hometown. Our world became smaller and smaller.

Eventually, we went on fewer and fewer outings in our hometown. Fewer dinners out with friends. Fewer parties, since standing for long periods was very challenging. And then, less and less church. Finally, totally confined in our home.

You are probably feeling sad for me by now. Don't! It wasn't sad. These final months were a very special time in our marriage. I guess the shrinks would call it acceptance. John accepted, with great grace, what was happening to his body. I did my best to follow suit. I'm not certain that my stiff upper lip served me well—at least not after John was gone. I would estimate that in seven years I probably cried less than ten times, maybe even less than seven. I suppressed the tears. I did that to honor the brave stance John had taken in facing the end of his life. I suppressed my emotions so long that it became natural to me. In death, I was stoic. I didn't cry the night he died. Nor the next day at the funeral home. I hardly cried at his funeral. The next two weeks were Christmas, which I spent with my children and grandchildren. Again, no tears. I saw the furtive glances at me. They all wondered where the tears were.

They came at last. I was driving home from Christmas and was twenty-five miles from home when they began. They did not end for eight months. I cried every day for eight months. I cried first thing in the morning when I looked at the single cup next to the coffeemaker. Each day was awash with remembrances from a life that was no more.

A friend, someone who cares deeply, opined that she was surprised that I was experiencing so much grief since I had known for such a long time that this time would come. I certainly had enough time to become adjusted to what was occurring. You probably already know—it doesn't work that way. Loss of presence is everything! I've spoken with many widows and we all agreed. We would take our mates back just like they were—sick as they may have been. But no, I would not have wished that on him! Having him back sick would have been very selfish, even if that was an option.

I do think that the way I made it through the first few months of grief was that I negotiated with God. *If You will just let him return for thirty minutes a week, I can do this.* As the weeks passed, I began to say, "If he can just come back one more time, I will be okay." Then, one day, after I shared my desire with a friend, she said, "Oh, if he comes back, will you call us?" I laughed and said, "If he comes back, I'll call the media!" I never said it again. The negotiation had served its purpose. I had made it through those first horrible months. I had made it to that point even though I was still a long way from the finish line.

The bad news is that I don't think there is a finish line. I say that with shocking clarity. Death is a scar that never quite heals. You never know when something will quite suddenly rip the scab off and the tears will flow again. Even after nearly six years there are things that will bring the tears—not often, and not for long, but there they are, and I am never prepared!

My belief is that the negotiating we do with God is another attempt to control the situation. In many ways our life seemed "under control" before this horrible loss; loss of life equals loss of control. Most of us know that there are few things we can control. We come to understand that in full color when death knocks at our door. Negotiating with God is one of the ways we continue to try to retain control. Others are illustrated in the words "if only" and "what if?" We will discuss those later. How can it be that our perfect plan has a huge hole right in the middle of it? A hole that cannot be repaired. There must be something I "should have" done to prevent this unimaginable, horrific event. After all, it is my job as a spouse, or parent, or—fill in the blank—to prevent this. Certainly, I should have done something, anything, but alas, there was nothing that could be done.

Not one of us can see into the future. Not one of us can predict the future. If we could, so many things would be different. Would we all live forever? Would there be no accidents? Would we live in perfection? When it is put that way, we see it differently. Bottom line is that the past is non-negotiable. Try as we may we are unable to change past events. Recognize that bargaining is one of Elisabeth Kubler-Ross' recognized stages of grief. We will do it to one extent or another. All those stages of grief are common to us as humans, and moreover, helpful in our healing.

We have all heard stories about foxhole religion. Foxhole religion could be described as someone in a foxhole with bullets flying over his or her head who says to God, "If you are real and if you save my life today, I promise that I will spend the rest of my days honoring you with my life." Just how many of those promises kept are unknown to any but the promiser—and God. That is negotiating with God! When we are in a mess and those around us have no power to save us, we appeal to a higher power. I would guess that it's been going on throughout time. In my case, I did not expect God to send my husband back to earth! However, it was a great vehicle to get me through those first darkest, hopeless days. Also, it makes a great story now!

I tell these stories because I realize if you too are going through grief and loss, it is helpful to look at what you are experiencing and feel "normal." It is important to know that however you approach grieving if okay. Many things are "common" as we deal with loss. My experience of grief can be a word picture that comforts. I share not to say this is the "right" way or the only way, but to say this is how I walked through grief. You will create your own path. Be secure that there is no "right" way.

Cathy's Story

My friend Cathy says she did a lot of negotiating with God during the death of two of her children. Her first loss was an eighteen-month-old child who died in a one-car accident in which Cathy was driving.

If you have ever driven with a toddler in the car, you know how overwhelming it can be to hear them crying while you are trying to focus. There is a lot of news coverage today about texting and driving, and we have all seen someone doing it. We see women putting on their makeup, especially mascara, and we see people eating fast food as they drive. I confess that I have done some of those at times in my life. I don't know if it's the news coverage or perhaps I have matured (it's time) enough to realize that the message can't be that important, or the makeup, or the hamburger. In only a moment our lives can be changed—FOREVER.

That is what happened to my friend Cathy. The loss of a baby coupled with the feeling of responsibility could drag any one of us down. Cathy grieved and was able to not grow bitter or to beat herself up to a degree that she was unable to forgive herself and carry on her life. I'll say that you must have a strong constitution to be able to do what Cathy did. She is a person of strong faith, and she relied on her faith to get her through the darkest times.

The loss of a fifteen-year-old was much harder for her to walk through. Cathy left the house and it would appear that her son, Ryan, died almost immediately from some type of loss-of-oxygen incident, according to the autopsy, an asthmatic event. Cathy's mother was to bring Ryan to the stadium for a marching festival. How horrible to discover a child dead who was getting ready to go marching with the band! So very traumatizing. He was not ill. He was in great health—in good enough condition to march with the band on a hot afternoon.

Cathy would have never allowed Ryan to march if he were not feeling well. Cathy wanted answers. Cathy needed answers. And of course, others wanted answers too. The problem with other people asking questions is that it feels like an indictment! We imagine we hear inferences in questions that may or may not exist. The negotiating with God and the "if only" and "what ifs?" circle in a vicious vortex of accusations coming from deep within. How could this happen? God, why? Why? Why? How can I parent my other children when I have lost this one? Can I trust myself? Can I trust God?

I report to you today that Cathy is one of the most well-adjusted people I know. Her faith has brought her to this point. It was not an easy journey. She worked through the pain, the loss, the self-analysis until...until she was able to make peace with two events that still take my breath away to even consider. We must work until.... We must pursue all avenues of healing until we are healed. One of those avenues for Cathy was to join Compassionate Friends, which is an organization for parents who have lost children. She worked until.... Now she tells her story in faith and confidence that she will be able to help someone else.

Sadly, Cathy will neither be the first nor the last to experience such a depth of loss. The work she did to recover will, however, benefit someone else along the way.

Key Points

1. Grieving often begins at diagnosis.
2. Try to spend more time in the present than dreading the future or reliving and regretting the past.
3. Hang on to whatever gives you comfort, even if it is something of a hope or a dream more than a reality.

Moving Forward

Negotiating or bargaining is a common part of grieving. Use it as a tool to get you through the darkest hours!

Why Am I So Damn Mad?

Anger is an ugly emotion. None of us enjoy being angry. Yet, Kubler-Ross reports anger as one of the stages of grief. One of the emotions that we will almost certainly go through when we experience grief. I hate that. Oops, my anger is showing!

Years ago, a very close friend's husband was in the early stages of Alzheimer's disease. On a Saturday evening my husband and I had dinner with this couple and had such a fun evening. At that time, our friend was experiencing some symptoms—he couldn't tell a story without help and he couldn't calculate the check and pay it—but these were not serious enough to impede a memorable evening. We laughed and looked back on memories of other dinners and trips we had taken and enjoyed together over the years.

Two days later, he found the keys to his car and went for a drive. He had lived there all his life, but with his new challenges, he drove down a one-way street going the opposite way! The outcome, as one would imagine, was not good. Fortunately, no one else was injured, if you don't count the bank that got a new drive-thru window! As for him, he had a broken hip that required surgery. Anesthesia has damaging effects to a brain already dealing with Alzheimer's. And, his dementia took a turn for the worse—not in small part to the anesthesia, but also because of the time spent in the hospital away from his familiar circumstances. I was shocked at the anger of his wife. I had never seen her be without compassion. At the time I was appalled at her anger. Not now. I'm all too familiar with the anger that comes with grief.

A car accident is not a death. Yet, that relatively minor car accident changed their lives and exponentially accelerated the speed of the Alzheimer's symptoms. Her anger was toward the loss of time ripped from their lives.

In my own life, I experienced anger upon the diagnosis of John's illness. John was ill for seven years, and I didn't recognize that anger until after his death. Looking back on that time, I would say that I was only angry for a few months or even weeks. My anger was because he was going to die. How could he leave me!

And, more poignantly, my anger was because of the death of our hopes and dreams. One by one I saw dreams clawed away. John and I were in the process of planning a retirement home, a second home in an area we loved. As soon as he was diagnosed, we stopped the plans for the house. We knew that he had to be near medical facilities. It was that simple. There were not significant facilities in the area we were planning our home.

Our losses came slowly. The rules to fly with oxygen were to make your plans sixty days in advance. There goes spontaneity. Paperwork had to be signed and submitted with the reservation. That meant mailing the forms to his doctor in Dallas, then to the oxygen provider in our city, and finally to the airline. All these things had to be accomplished sixty days prior to travel. (I understand that the procedures have been simplified, but at the time, those were the rules.)

John and I loved the Oregon coast and planned a trip there to escape the heat of the desert in August. Unfortunately, our flight had a delayed departure and, then, we circled forty-five minutes before landing in Portland. John and I both were trying hard not to watch the digital readout on the oxygen machine. It was as if you could hear the seconds ticking away. Neither of us had a clue what would happen if the oxygen supply was exhausted. How quickly would the lack of sufficient oxygen be a problem? Would the airline provide oxygen in an emergency? Would he DIE or lose consciousness? Perhaps have organ damage? How dire would the consequences be for diminished oxygen? When we landed, there were only minutes left on the meter. Nerve-racking beyond explanation! With no conversation about the subject, we never took another trip by air.

Anger is a response to another emotion. Often, I would say that anger is a response to fear. For certain, my response to the news that John had a terminal condition was fear. Admittedly, mostly fear for me. How can I live without him? What will my life be like living alone?

Anger toward God is a common response. Why be mad at someone local when you can go straight to the top? It's okay to be mad at God. It will not solve your problems, but this anger born from fear takes time to digest. Time is our friend in healing from grief, and the same can be said of healing from whatever anger and angst exists in your heart.

Anger toward the doctors. Doctors can be very frustrating. A great many doctors focus all their energy on total healing. However, when someone is suffering from a terminal illness, the focus needs to be on quality of life rather than quantity of years. The caregiver must make difficult decisions that would be easier if the doctor would focus on giving the patient comfort and quality of life rather than a longer life.

I hear anger in the question *Why?* Why is this happening to us now? He retired last month, and now he is dying! Why was my mate taken in a horrific accident? Why did his heart just stop? He was a lifetime exerciser!

The question of why is usually a question of control. We all desire control. During these times of grief, we realize we have no control. We had a plan for our life. It was a perfectly good plan. Why now? Control, when there is none. Now, the fear increases because something else bad can happen. No one is safe. I've lost control.

Anger in families. When families are dysfunctional, it is not uncommon for the dysfunction to increase during a severe illness. As a chaplain, I have heard it said again and again, "Can't Susie just get along through this really hard time?" The truth is if Susie has never had the tools to be calm and get along in a crisis, she is not going to suddenly find the ability to do so now. Not now with the increased stress and uncertainty! You must realize that you can only control your own actions and reactions. Dave Kuhnert, in his book *Servant Leadership*, says that there are only three things you can control: who you trust, how you act, and your perspective.

Anger, fear, the loss of control, or whatever other label you put on it, those emotions will be a part of the grieving process. Adopt a perspective that accepts your loss, gigantic though it may be. Work through your anger, accepting that it is a common emotion during grief. Acceptance is a large step in the process of getting beyond anger.

I go back to what Dave Kuhnert says about being able to control only three things. I put my trust in God; I make certain my actions are honorable; and I adopt a perspective that tells me I still live on this earth even though part of me has now died. I have things to accomplish here and I have people I still love here. It only makes sense in the light of those things to work at healing my heart and to continue to make a contribution in this short time we have.

In his book *Yellow Balloons,* Tim Dunn says that our life is like a two-minute ride at the amusement park. It's exhilarating, and we need to throw ourselves fully into it before it ends. We must try to find a perspective that allows us to grieve, heal, and go on to use the lessons we learn during these trials of life.

The biggest problem with anger is when it is not resolved. An extremely successful man who owned a national chain of restaurants, Joe, was a man of great faith. His forty-year-old wife of less than six years was diagnosed with breast cancer. The couple had two young sons who grew into men of great faith like their mother and their dad had, at one time. Unfortunately, Joe never let go of his anger at God. He died a few years ago. He was still angry and had never recovered the faith that would have helped him walk through the devastation of his grief.

By contrast, I also have a friend who lost her husband in an auto accident when they were in their early thirties. She raised their two young daughters and remarried a few years later. Her life has been good and productive, filled with both the pain of loss of her first dreams and the joy of fulfillment in a new forty-year marriage. She had no time for anger, and she was able to fully walk in a new relationship and have an extremely productive life.

The bottom line is that we all choose. No one else chooses for us. We alone decide whether to be bitter or to recover. The decision is not an easy one. However, the decision is one that affects the remainder of our life. Work at healing. Work through your anger. Get counseling. Talk about your grief. Don't hide it or stuff your feelings deep inside your heart. If you have suffered the loss of someone you love, grief is your new job. A job as important as any you will ever have. Don't shrink from it! Don't hide! Lean into your grief! In doing so, you may be the strongest you will ever need to be!

Sandy and Tommy's Story

Sandy and Tommy were certainly people who had every reason to be angry at life—angry at God. They were people of faith and had lived out their faith in their day-to-day lives for forty-plus years. Life seemed perfect except that their son had married a girl from Tennessee and moved away. They saw Jimmy and his family a couple of times a year, but Jimmy's wife, Teresa, didn't enjoy Oklahoma and visited as little as possible. When their two boys were born, Sandy and Tommy made the trek to Tennessee a few times a year. They wanted to know their grandchildren!

They received one of those middle-of-the-night phone calls that we all dread but few of us ever receive. The call informed them that there had been a boating accident. Jimmy and one of the boys had died. Teresa and the other boy had survived. An enormous tragedy. Sandy and Tommy left immediately for Tennessee—even though their daughter, Linda, was in the hospital having her second daughter.

Sandy and Tommy were gone for a week. Their entire lives changed in that very short week. They returned to find that their daughter, Linda, only surviving child now, had been diagnosed with breast cancer before she was discharged from the maternity unit of the hospital.

Life was complicated. There was no time to grieve. Their only son and one grandson were now dead, and their only daughter was now fighting breast cancer. The next two years were a maze. From the sidelines you could witness the frenetic activity. The fight for the life of a mother combined with help for the day-to-day needs of a two-year-old and a new baby kept both Sandy and Tommy busy daily. They were on the front lines of a battle for the life of a daughter, a mother, a wife. They fought hard.

There is always a winner and a loser in every war. Linda lost her war after two years.

Now Sandy and Tommy's days and nights were taken up with assisting their son-in-law in raising their granddaughters. After only six months, he remarried. They were stunned, and frankly, worried about what the future would bring.

I watched as they grieved for their now deceased children and the life that had once been so "regular" and now was fractured and had little resemblance to the peaceful life of previous years. The question was, "Are you angry?" "Angry that your daughter isn't cold in her grave and her husband has remarried?" The quiet answer was, "What else can I do but accept this? How would anger help? I could lose the only family we have left."

Thirty-five years have passed now. The son-in-law and his new wife adopted Sandy and Tommy. Three more children were born into their new family. The children are all grandchildren with no differences made between them. This is a sweet ending to a tragedy that a lot of people would be unable to recover from. Certainly, anger would have been an easy response!

Key Points

1. Anger is a normal response to loss.
2. Anger is generally a response to another emotion.
3. Recognize your anger and work hard to resolve it quickly.

Moving Forward

Understand that anger is often a response to loss. Analyze your anger and be honest with yourself about your feelings. Talk with a counselor, a friend, or a member of the clergy to get help in expressing your anger in appropriate ways to those you love.

Do the
Next Thing

I have heard so many stories about things that a widow has never encountered before. For me, the first was social security. I literally got a letter from them daily for two weeks. They wanted to know if I wanted to continue to receive an amount that did/did not include waiting for some future date when I could receive a larger check. First, I was amazed that they were contacting me so quickly after the death. But, holy moly, people, don't send me a letter daily. It felt like stalking!

The letters were made more confusing by the fact—and this is not hyperbole—each letter gave me a different amount than any of the previous letters!

How can one be expected to decide with details that change daily! It was like herding cats! Finally, I went to a meeting with the Social Security Administration. Again, they gave me yet another figure! I had another meeting with them before I made my decision. When asked by my son what I had decided, I replied, "No decision. No decision is a decision." The problem with social security is that if one decides to receive the amount, that is a firm, unchangeable decision. A decision not to receive the money was a decision that gave me a little grace—time to consult with others, time to see how my finances were going.

I knew a widow who was attempting to wade through all the legal details of widowhood. She closed all her joint credit card accounts and opened new ones under only her name. She was very proud at the steps that she had taken to be transparent to those companies whose credit cards she possessed and used. A few months later she found that her credit was damaged because she had "applied" for so much credit! Now, she did not need to apply for any credit for anything at that time, but she was devastated that she had done something in good faith that had turned out in such a negative way.

The bottom line for widows is to seek legal advice. Seek advice from trusted friends or from clergy. Then, when you decide, trust it. You have not lost your mind, even though you may feel as if you have.

You may need to take a little more time and to make decisions more slowly. Most people (institutions) are going to allow you more time in this situation—not all, but most.

Unfortunately, I sought legal advice that was marginal, at best. My husband and I had not changed our legal representative when we moved three hundred miles away. With modern technology, it is easy to do business from remote locations. HOWEVER, in Texas the law that pertained to me in death was that the estate would have to be probated even though there was a will. Probate requires a local attorney who can go to the county offices several times. The expense of paying an attorney to fly in and take care of those duties would have been ridiculous. So, my out-of-town representative referred me to someone he had known in law school. Without giving too many boring details, this guy was not competent and spent a great amount of time on the phone with me, which, of course, I was being billed for. Most all these calls were initiated by the attorney.

While I realized I was being billed, I was still fragile and not ready to be as forceful as was needed. In the end he billed me for an exorbitant amount of money. I was quite unhappy, but no one was willing to advise me what to do. As I said previously, *insecurity* was the word of the season for me. I summoned my courage by tapping into my anger and the injustice of the moment. You have the same mind you had prior to the death of your husband. Use it!

I sent a payment for approximately one-quarter of what I was billed and wrote on the check "full and final payment." I knew that if he cashed the check, he had just accepted full and final payment. Along with the payment I sent a letter detailing all the questionable charges and my desire to put this behind me, but that I was certainly willing to share with others the details of the letter if I needed to do so to close the transaction. Then, I waited. Six weeks later, the check was cashed. I did it! My self-confidence was bolstered over the top because I had used the brain that had sustained me up until that point!

A member of the widow's group that I facilitate purchased a new home. Her story is heartbreaking. I'll call her Sharon. Sharon and her husband moved to our city in November of the previous year to be near their son. The following February, her husband died. While his health had some challenges, he died rather unexpectantly. I met her in May only a few months into her grief. I took her to dinner to get acquainted and she told me she was quite happy living in her small apartment when I inquired about when she would purchase property. I hated to be the bearer of bad news, but in our city during the current "oil boom," the problem with apartments is that they tend to raise the rent by hundreds of dollars each time you renew. The only way to stabilize rent is to quit paying it! Purchase property—in a market where everything is overpriced!

Sharon called me the following day to relate that she had called the manager of the apartment complex to find that her current apartment unit was leasing for $500 more than she was currently paying for it! She could see that her rent would be raised by at least that amount when her lease renewed, and perhaps even more. Sharon began seeking to purchase a property for a price that would seem moderate anywhere else, but in our current "boom," which resulted in a great demand for real estate, the prices were not all that comfortable for her budget. As widows, lots of us are on fixed incomes, and we realize that we must control our expenses and be wise with the money we do have. In lots of cases it must last the remainder of our lives.

Sharon's mantra was "I can't do this." She felt ill-equipped to purchase a home when her head was still muddled. I can remember not being able to decide on a menu selection at that early time and couldn't imagine being forced to make such an enormous decision. And yet, the smartest thing for Sharon to do was to make this decision now and not be forced to face this when her rent increased to some new painful high.

I am happy to report that Sharon did find an
appropriate home. She overcame her insecurities
and made a decision. Her confidence was restored.
She made that decision by enlisting the help of her
son and daughter-in-law and new friends from our
group. Sharon did exactly what I am advising: Use
the resources you have—family, friends, financial
counselors, but most of all your own savvy! Decision
made, there were still many overwhelming decisions to make—the logistics of moving, restoration
of the new home before moving in, and dealing
with workmen.

I can't count the number of times that someone
has said to me, "I can't do this." Missionary Elisabeth
Elliott's husband was killed by the very people to
whom they were attempting to minister. After his
death, instead of running for the hills or the safety
of home back in the US, Elisabeth stayed on to complete her martyred husband's mission. She was coura-
geous on so many levels! She said that when she felt
she did not know what to do next she would say to
herself, "Do the next thing."

That statement is good advice. We do not have to
face anything but this moment! Scripture reinforces
this message when it says "each day has enough trouble
(or worry) for itself." (Matt. 6:34) Try hard to live in
the moment. Handle tomorrow (and the future) as it

comes. And when, in the middle of the day you don't know what to do next, do the next thing.

Many times, it is the difference between the spray of a shotgun or the narrow focus of a rifle. We must narrow our focus so that we may identify the next tiny step instead of being overwhelmed by the blank canvas that resembles our life. We don't know whether to pick up the small or large brush; to use the primary colors or the pastel; acrylic or watercolors. Don't force a decision on the big picture but focus on the next small thing you can identify. In time those tiny pieces will begin to show a new picture.

Those of us who are married, both women and men, tend to divvy up the responsibilities of life. I know older women who know absolutely nothing about their finances. I know men who are unable to do laundry. If you are a couple who has means, it is true that you can hire someone to do laundry and the accounting. Those are still things to acquaint yourself with during marriage—before the crisis!

I have included an appendix of useful information. Share this list with others or, better yet, complete it for the one who will be facing these questions when/ if you should die suddenly! Know where your important papers are now kept. Store them in a safe place and let someone know their location. List names of attorneys, doctors, and clergy who might be helpful. Add someone as a joint account holder onto your bank account now, so that in the event of your own death, the accounts are not locked down awaiting probate or whatever legal formalities exist in your state. Reorganize the files and important information into systems that are friendly to you. Simply moving the most-used files to a more easily accessed drawer position seems very small, but don't make yourself stand on a ladder to reach things that can be accessed readily by you from a lower shelf. It is yours now!

Janie and Dan's Story

Fun could have been part of their names, Janie and Dan. They laughed and teased and worked hard at their relationships with friends. Janie had flawless olive skin and perfect hair. Don's hair was white, almost silver. They laughed and teased and worked hard at their relationships with friends. They called to check on you; made time in their busy schedule for dinners and trips. They were a part of both the good times and the bad. One never knew what would show up on your porch—once a croaking frog animated by movement showed up on ours the day of a big family party. For over thirty years, we were close friends. We knew each other's children and shared the obstacles of life.

Dan had a congenital heart problem, and even though he ran almost daily and focused on good health, he was fragile. Janie was healthy, almost never ill. For years they prepared for his death—powers of attorney, living wills, legal wills, codicils, the gamut of all things legal so that she would know exactly what to do when he died.

Unfortunately, God doesn't always follow the well-thought-out plans of man. One day Janie said that she was having indigestion problems and had been for a while. She finally put off some committee appointments and a day of golf and got in to see a gastrointestinal doctor. He began to run a series of tests and came back within a few days with a diagnosis—pancreatic cancer. Terminal. Her days were short. In fact, almost from the beginning, she became quite ill. Janie had chemo and was receiving the finest medical care you could get, but it looked as if the doctor's grim prognosis was going to be correct. She could not keep food down, chemo was challenging, and even though she tried to be upbeat, we all felt like we could see how this was going to end. Janie died four months later.

Dan felt as if his heart had stopped. He was lost. All the preparations made for his death were wasted time. He was alive and Janie was gone. Even though he was prepared in a legal way, he was not prepared for Janie to die first. He was certain that he would die and that he had covered all the bases. He was not prepared for the hours of loneliness that ensued. He loved the dog, but Janie had always taken care of it. And, truth be told, Janie had spoiled the dog. Dan was grieving and dealing with a spoiled dog, who was also grieving. Everything was too much for his heart, and it stopped, permanently, only one year later.

That does not mean preparation is not good. It is good. Even when things do not go as planned.

Key Points

1. There are many unfamiliar personal business matters to face initially.
2. Even though it is a challenging time mentally and emotionally, trust your ability to make decisions.
3. It is sometimes better to put off a decision than to make a rash decision.

Moving Forward

Spend time educating yourself on the business of your life.

* * *

For those of you who do not live in an economy based on oil production, an oil boom is when things are going well in the oil fields and production is at its highest. Our streets are flooded with new people who come to the area to work. Unskilled workers can draw salaries beginning at $22 an hour and work as much as 100 hours a week. Everything else suffers, such as our roads because of all the oil field trucks. Our schools experience overcrowding; our restaurants can't find wait staff (long waits—two hours—for dinners out); and lines become endlessly long at the car wash, pharmacy, etc. Doctors, dentists, lawyers, and veterinarians all decide to close their practice to new clients and serve the clients they currently have. The worst part is the prices go sky-high. The cost of living is totally over the top.

Unfortunately, usually after a boom comes a bust. A bust is characterized by lots of for-sale signs on homes, fewer cars at red lights, and, sadly, the closing of businesses. The majors (Exxon, Conoco, Shell, or whatever other large oil company) move out—usually back to Houston—and we become that sleepy little town again. The locals breathe a sigh of relief. After only twenty years I can testify that the booms last longer than the busts! Now, you have had a small economy lesson on the oil business and can better understand what it is like to be a widow in the Permian Basin.

Things Will Never Be the Same

The statement that is common to all of us—things changed in a moment. Things will never be the same. Yes, that's true, but the statement is also true of happy events—new marriage, new home, new exalted position at work, huge raise, graduating from college, winning the Nobel Prize. However, as humans we rarely reflect on the changes that appear to be positive. We only bemoan the negative ones.

Research says that the positive things that occur in our lives cause stress on our bodies as do negative ones. The Holmes-Rahe test, which was developed in 1976 by two psychiatrists, lists forty-three common life events including marriage, divorce, death, and such minor events as major holidays. They have analyzed the results by a simple answer of yes or no to whether you have experienced any of the forty-three events. At the high end, the results indicate if you could be on the road to illness because of stress. Surprisingly, happy, joyful events can give you stress. Unsurprisingly, death of a spouse is at the top of the scale for stressful life events. If you have lost your spouse, you already know this.

Things do change in a moment. And, yes, you can never go back to the way things were before. We are now in search of a new normal. At first you will reject the very idea of a new normal. At first you are still in denial, or even anger, and do not desire acceptance. Acceptance is where you are going, but it's not a place to begin.

You are in a place where your only option is to walk through the pain. Your life will be a maze at the beginning. A maze of railing, either silently or audibly. In the maze you will run into disbelief; total loss of ability to think and focus; negotiating with God to bring back your spouse; and longing for what you had. This is a time when your loved one may be elevated to a new high, faultless, blameless, perfect. A place where no human can survive and certainly doesn't belong. It is easy to fall into a place where our memory deceives us into thinking that everything was perfect. Let's be honest, things were never perfect. The fact is that we would take our spouse back, imperfect as they might be!

Back to reality. Reality says that our relationship was not perfect because two imperfect people were involved. Elevating your spouse beyond the clouds just serves to keep you in a place of denial, which is not healthy. This is probably not your biggest problem now but try to recognize that this is an easy trap to fall into.

At some point you will need to accept the truth that your life will never be the same. The good news is that you are more in charge of who you become than you have ever been before.

The first step is acceptance of the death. This will take some time and that will be different for each person. It could take several years. I have witnessed two kinds of responses. One seems to be holding onto the grief as if it is a friend. By wrapping oneself in suffering, you can deny the comfort that may come your way. It is exhausting to your friends and family; i.e., your support system. Grieving is not a choice. I don't want to insinuate that it is. Grief is the natural response to the loss of someone you love. Many things will affect that. Age, length of relationship, even gender. But, at some point you must move from denial. Denial is not a place to spend your life.

The other type of person is the person who seems to accept almost from the beginning that his or her spouse will not return and that the individual must make a new life. I wish I could fully delineate the reason for the difference. If that could be bottled and sold, much suffering could be avoided!

Of course, there are the folks who go back and forth between the two spheres. I would guess that most of grieving falls into this category. Outwardly, I seemed to belong in the latter group, but when I was alone, I spent time denying the obvious truth. Maybe we could call this the wishful category. I think most of us spend some time wishing this terrible truth was different. Hoping to wake from this nightmare.

As you engage in the world again, you will find that you still have a sense of humor— that is, if you had one before! You will probably be appalled that you can still laugh. Laughter and joy are emotions that you don't know how to handle now. They seem so foreign considering the dark place of your soul. Laugh anyway. Everything you do will feel awkward, so enjoy the lightness that you feel when you begin to find the humor in life again. For me, it seemed like my feelings changed rapidly and I never quite knew which place my feelings would land. I knew that I was not in charge of them. Indeed, they were in charge of me!

What I am trying to tell you here is that there is no right way or wrong way. There is only where you are in a moment. If you find that you are stuck in a terribly bad place, counseling is often the key. Bouncing ideas off another person can help you analyze the thoughts better. My thoughts were often a merry-go-round. I had a couple of counseling sessions. I had never lost someone close to me, so I needed some guidance. Don't condemn yourself if you need help. Having someone tell you that you are not losing your mind can be so helpful. This is common to what you are going through. Don't be averse to help. Maybe clergy is the answer, or even just a member of your support group. Ask. That is the best next step.

No, things will never be the same. Now is the time to begin molding the next season of your life. You can now approach things from a different, more thoughtful, and even more selfish point of view. Now is the time to focus on you. Think about some of the past New Year's resolutions. Now could be a good time to begin implementing some of those into your life.

The key is NOW! Now is where you are. You hope to never be at this place again. But, for now, you are here. Lean into your grief. Don't deny your tears. Cry them. They will eventually diminish. Cry them rather than suppress them. Suppressed tears eventually must be cried. You will never cry them all. Your broken heart will mend, but there will be times when the bandage will be suddenly ripped off and the tears will come again. This just means you loved the person a lot! Don't flinch; it's a common occurrence!

At the beginning of your grief, you will feel dead on the inside. Dead like the tree looks in winter. Bare. Cold. Without hope. Think of those first tiny leaves in spring. You will be like that in time. Those tiny new leaves will represent hope. Each leaf represents something new in your life. A part of the new picture. The new season.

I have a six-foot bougainvillea that I always bring into the house for the winter. The year that John died I neglected to bring it in. I was too encompassed by the dying going on indoors to be concerned with the dying going on outdoors. After John's death, I looked outside to see that the bougainvillea had lost all its leaves in a frost. At first, I did not care, but I finally had it brought in. I had little hope that it would survive, but I was giving it a chance. One day I looked at it and saw tiny little bugs crawling on the branches. Oh, good grief! One more thing to deal with! Upon closer examination, I found that tiny new leaves were popping out, not bugs! I smiled. I felt like God had sent me a message that I too would have new life. Maybe not now, but in time. Hope. A sign of hope.

Look for signs of hope. You will find them in smiles, in invitations, in an unsuppressed giggle with a friend. Life will continue. Be a part of it. You will feel awkward at first. You have lost part of yourself. A part of yourself that you worked hard to develop. The oneness of marriage. Your new focus is to find a new oneness. The oneness of you! Make yourself whole again. You have heard it said that "life is for the living," and it is true. You are alive. You are meant to be a part of life again. Life is full and includes joy and pain, suffering and healing. This may be the hardest thing you have ever healed from, but you can do it.

Edith and Harmon's Story

Edith was eighty-six; Harmon was eighty-seven. They had been married sixty-nine years. They lived on the same lovely farm for over sixty years. He no longer farmed but often used the tractor to mow or do other odd jobs on the farm. They leased the land to a young neighbor with a family. They leased it to him for a nominal amount. Harmon and Edith no longer had a need for a lot of income, and they both received a great deal of joy from the young Hanks family. Harmon passed along tips for rotating crops to Joe Bob, while Edith provided canning tips to Mary. The neighborhood children loved to come over and help with the livestock chores after school. Both families benefited from the other generation. After school Edith could often be found making cookies or homemade donuts in the winter. The children would often get off the bus to enjoy the goodies before going home.

The story was beautiful until the day that Harmon stood up on the tractor to look at a fox scamper across the pasture. No one will ever know what made him lose his balance and fall under the tractor. Edith was making lunch and only began to worry when the clock showed 12:15. Harmon was never late for lunch. He would stop mowing in time to be in the house by straight-up noon. Edith went outside to check on Harmon and saw the tractor. She could hear it idling but could not see Harmon anywhere. She began to run. At eight-six Edith could still move her legs at a fair clip. Thankfully, the tractor was in the field nearest the house. Edith needed to stop and get her breath, but her adrenaline pushed her forward. As she crossed the newly plowed furrows, she could see Harmon pinned under the plow. Panicked, she called out to him but got no answer. His breathing was shallow, but he was still breathing. About that time Edith saw Joe Bob driving down the dirt road. She took off her apron and flagged him down. Joe Bob used his cell phone to call for help. Edith slumped down next to Harmon and caressed his face and spoke softly to him.

The week went by quickly. Edith never left the hospital. She stayed at Harmon's bedside night and day. Harmon never rallied. He slipped into a coma on day three and then slipped into eternity on day four.

Edith and Harmon had no children. They had lived on this beautiful little farm for over sixty years now. The Hanks family helped Edith get through this crisis as best as they could. Edith went about the business of death, taking care of the necessary legal paperwork after the funeral. Then one day a couple of weeks after Harmon's death, Mary went to check on Edith and found her slumped in her rocking chair on the back porch. Edith could not go on without Harmon. Life would never be the same and Edith could not endure life without him.

Key Points

1. Things will never be the same.
2. Don't listen to people who do not understand your circumstances.
3. Ignore insensitive comments that people make to you.

Moving Forward

Look for signs of hope. Buy into the future.

Questions
Questions
Questions

You will find as you take the journey of caregiving, the death of a loved one, and the
search for healing that you face many questions. Many firsts. One of the conundrums that I
still face is who to celebrate with when something
wonderful occurs. We can all make it through the
difficult times. We have had plenty of practice by
living through the death of someone dear. But what
do you do when something amazing takes place?
Some achievement that you have worked hard to see
come to fruition. Who do you tell? Your dog? I love

my dog, but she has yet to say a word that encouraged me! I know this subject seems minor and I agree that it is. However, it speaks to the loneliness of living alone.

Have you had your first bout of illness since the loss of your mate? When you wake up with laryngitis, what do you do? You figure it out. Most of us would rather do something for someone else than to have something done for us. During the past two years I had three orthopedic surgeries. Recovery was a nightmare. I felt so alone. I was alone. I made it through none the worse for wear, but there were days when I had a pity party.

Can you reach everything you need to reach? I can't. I can do most things. I can change most of my lightbulbs in my high ceilings. Outside I have one light that is impossible even with a ladder. It's impossible. I tried early on and fell off the ladder into the boxwoods. I lay there and laughed. My dog thought I was losing it. She stood over me looking down as I laughed heartily.

Do you dread the holidays now? After we get past that first year of "firsts," you can feel so lost. If your own father is deceased, Father's Day is pretty much a non-starter once your husband is gone. Valentine's Day is just a reminder that you are alone! I learned, the hard way, that I don't want to spend holidays alone. Next year I will go out of town, maybe take a cruise. Or a day trip. Being at home is a poignant reminder that you are alone. Take control!

Do you have a support system to answer questions that fall out of your expertise? Taxes. Purchasing a new car. Or home. One night when I went out and returned after dark, I came home to total blackness outside my home. I found that all my outdoor lights were not working. I was very surprised as I looked at a home that was totally dark. My home looked deserted! I realized that I had no idea how long the lights had been out. I wasn't accustomed to coming home after dark and so this was a small detail that I had overlooked. And, I must say for safety's sake, outdoor lighting is necessary!

What do you do when the alarm goes off in the night? It's something that will happen sooner or later. Or, if you don't have an alarm, that sound in the night that scares the bejeebers out of you. Do you have a neighbor you can call? Make a plan.

Does a neighbor or friend have your house key? If you get locked out, you need to have someone to help you get in. You don't want to call a locksmith. They are expensive. I installed a key pad outside my garage door. It was inexpensive and I don't know how many times I have needed it!

Does a neighbor have an emergency number to call, a family member, if there is an emergency when you are not home? I took a road trip to see my son about a month after the death of my husband. As I was getting ready to leave, I realized that there was no one who knew who to call in case of an accident. I could visualize a state trooper standing at my front door ringing my bell. I put a small piece of paper in my wallet and in my car that says, "In case of emergency, call _____." It's such a small thing but could really be important!

Are you strong? Physically strong. I had to learn how to buy things in sizes that I could manage. I have a very large dog, and dog food is cheaper when purchased in large quantities. That became quite a challenge. I learned that price was less important than being able to manage and get it into the house!

Can you pick up the dog? Oh my, that was a huge challenge! I love big dogs. My labradoodle weighs eighty-one pounds. When she had a hip problem and needed to see the vet, I had to call someone to put her into my car and take her out again when I got home. I hated it, but it was impossible for me to lift her.

Can or will you go to church alone? Or are there other places you hate to go alone? It is not uncommon for widows or widowers to hate going to church or other places where they have gone for years. Parties are especially hard. We were so accustomed to doing that as a couple. Do we stop going? NO! It is important not to leave the relationships you have spent years building. Push past the awkwardness of being a "third wheel" and find the friendships you enjoyed before. They still feel the same about you. *You* just feel differently about *you*!

Can you do laundry? Most females can do laundry. However, if you are male you may not have had any reason to learn. It's a simple job. Get someone to go over the basics. Learn how to operate the machines and learn not to put the red sweatshirt in with the white underwear. Otherwise, you will be celebrating breast cancer month with pink underwear! And, on a lighter note, I once found a Spanish-speaking housekeeper spraying the collar of a shirt with bathtub cleaner—no more ring around the tub or the collar! (She mistook the bathroom cleaner for starch!)

Can you do the finances at your house? Write the checks? Keep up with the monthly bills? Know what is due when? Know when checks are direct deposited? These are important things that you should learn prior to the death of your loved one. Let him sit with you and look over your shoulder while you accomplish these tasks. You will be glad that you did.

Can you do all these things? Of course, you can do these and the gazillion other things you will face. Don't be discouraged and remember to celebrate the small victories!

Story of a State Funeral

On November 30, 2018, President George H. W.
Bush died at the age of ninety-four. As a country
we spent the better part of a week grieving corpo-
rately. Most news outlets spent some time daily
reporting on each new detail. Abundant attention
was paid to remembrance of all the many years
President Bush had given in service to our nation.
We fixed our eyes on the television and looked
back on the life of a man who loved his country and
loved his family. Much pomp and circumstance
accompanied the daily activities: Lying in state in
Texas. The entire family being transported by Air
Force One (loaned to the family by the current
president). Departures from air fields; arrivals
at other air fields. Lying in state in Washington.
Flying back to Texas. A train to his final resting
place. Various politicians reporting about times
past. Times of war. Times of peace.

During each of our lifetimes we will each experience any number of state funerals and, also, many
funerals in our own lives. The funerals we experience
are no less impactful without the pomp and circumstance. However, the state funerals reveal some
lessons to us that we can use for our own funerals.
One of the first things a president does in office is
to write his own obituary and plan his own funeral.

I was surprised to learn this fact. The Boy Scouts would simply say, "Be prepared." So, our first lesson is to be prepared.

The next thing we can observe from this type of flowery, formal service is to use this time with family and friends to celebrate the life that has ended. Perhaps your funeral service is not for a president in your family. But I am positive that there is much love for your family member, as we saw displayed by the members of President Bush's family. (I bet there is some dissension too.) Make a plan. Make certain the speakers are well acquainted with the deceased. And, I might also say, loved the deceased!

Make the service memorable. Make it a service that recognizes the personality of the deceased. Someone I know who was married to a farmer had his body taken from the church to the cemetery on a trailer pulled by a John Deere tractor. I feel certain that no one will ever erase that moment from their memories. Memorable is good because the ones left behind want to talk about the deceased. Be like a president and plan as much of the service as you can years in advance. You will not be sorry. If you yourself have ever had the responsibility to plan a service on a moment's notice, you fully understand the challenge of planning a funeral or memorial service.

Key Points

- Be prepared to face a lot of unknowns.
- Lean on others to help but learn to be empowered by gaining independence.
- Learn as much from your spouse before he/she passes.

Moving Forward

Assemble a support system that will address all the areas you recognize as out of your expertise. Challenge yourself to learn new things. You will feel empowered by new abilities!

If Only

If only I had gotten him to the hospital in time

If only I had him to help me make these decisions

If only the family understood

*If only I could move from this house
where we lived together*

If only I didn't have to move from this house

If only I could sleep

If only I had known he was going to die

If only I had been more prepared

If only he had lived until our daughter got married

If only he had lived until the children graduated

If only I had not said that "thing" the morning he died

If only I could see him one more time

If only I could kiss him goodbye

If only he could have reconciled with our oldest child

If only I had learned to run the business

If only I had learned more about our finances

If only we had tried another treatment

The "if onlies." A terrible place to live. A powerless place to live. We all tend to say, "if only." I think "if only" means "if only I was in control." Unfortunately, we are not in control. None of us—from the top executive to the manual laborer. Where does that leave us?

With a long list of regrets. Regret, along with guilt, is powerful, but not at all helpful in the healing process. We hear this proclamation at most tragedies.

We heard it after 9/11. We heard the stories of loved ones who had taken flights they were not scheduled for—and of those who were scheduled for flights that they didn't take, for whatever reason. If only...

The same thing could be said of the "what if?" statement. We can spend endless hours focusing on what we might have done or how things would have turned out if we had done something differently. This statement also renders us powerless. We don't get do-overs. That is a thing from the playground when we were children. A lot of time can be consumed with nothing gained by analyzing how we could have made a different decision that would have turned out differently.

I have a friend who lost both her husband and her only child in a horrific auto accident. The other driver was a drunk driver. Not only that, she was in the hospital for months. And now, three years later, she continues to have surgery and do rehab. Her loss is incomprehensible to me and to most of us. Recently we were talking about that horrifying day.

She related that they had been late leaving the house that day. Ah, if only they had left on time. (That is my statement, not hers. She has come to a place of acceptance through her faith.) However, I doubt that any of you can ignore the irony of the difference twenty minutes would have made in her life. Let me emphasize that acceptance is not a decision that you make in an instant. Acceptance comes over time.

The question now becomes: How do we get to acceptance? Synonyms for the word *acceptance: recognition of, acknowledgement of, acquiescence in, agreement with.* Wow. All those terms are unpalatable when what we are addressing is the death of someone we love.

Unpalatable though it might be, acceptance is the road to peace. At some point, either early on or after some time, acceptance should become your goal. As I mentioned previously, the word *widow* was a word I abhorred. I didn't want to be one and I didn't want to hang out with them! As time passed—not a few months, but a couple of years—I no longer hated the term. I accepted it. I made friends with the term. I learned to think of myself as a widow. I realized that a word does not define me. Widow is only a part of who I am. As time goes forward, it becomes a smaller dimension. Other things in my life are growing.

Do not misunderstand, I am not saying acceptance is easy or that it comes quickly. Time is your friend. The passage of time reminds us that life is precious. In time your heart will heal. Your loss will diminish but will still be there as you go forward. Earlier I related the comparison of the loss as a wound that we put a bandage over. At times we will remove the bandage and apply a balm to facilitate healing. Then, we bump that wound and it bleeds again. We cover it once more. Healing comes, but a scar is left. We all have scars that leave strong memories. The healing appears complete, but the scar remains. Leave behind the "if onlies" and seek to find new interests. Many things that are necessary are not easy. Try to not speak in absolutes. I'll never get over this. He will always be the only man I love. I'll never love again. And on and on. We have no idea what the future holds for us. And, that's a good thing! If we knew the future, we would have known of the impending loss we were facing! Try hard to live in the moment.

Many times, we will ourselves to move past our current thought patterns. I do this by thinking of something positive. Thinking about serving someone else. Taking those thoughts captive. Some days will be a pity party. We all do that, but you should try to not spend entire days there or at least entire weeks!

Try not to isolate yourself. Being with others helps. Be intentional about your healing. When negative thoughts come into your mind, turn the page. Go for a walk. Play with the dog. Call a friend. Take a seminar. Join a grief support group. Don't isolate yourself. Again, I say be intentional. Many of these things will have no interest for you. Life itself may have no interest to you, but you are still here for a reason.

Do your best to find your way in this new world you live in. This is not a world you would have chosen. It's the world you now live in. Death is a part of life; not the good part, but definitely a part. We are all going to go through this passage, and most of us more than once. There will be many losses. They can be financial. They can be as simple as an empty nest or as devastating as another death.

Sally's Story

A moment of great joy can change into the most tragic moment in only a second. A beautiful six-year-old child, Sally, had learned to ride a bicycle, and her mother had taken her to the bike shop to purchase her first new bike. It was pink with purple and pink ribbons streaming from the handlebars. She got on the bike and rode it around the parking lot, her blond hair blowing in the West Texas wind. A smile of pride covered her small face.

Her mother's car was too small to put the bike in so she told her daughter that her dad would pick it up and bring it home that afternoon. You can guess that the child was not at all pleased to have to wait several hours to ride her new bike in the neighborhood and show it off to all her friends. She begged. She pouted. She convinced her mom.

Sally rode her bike close to the curb, and Mom followed in the car. As they went down the hill near their home, Sally picked up speed. Sally's smile grew wider as she felt the wind in her face. She turned to see her mother's face, and because of her inexperience she turned the way she was looking and veered into the path of her mother's car. A brief life now ended.

I am certain the mother spent many lonely hours saying, "If only..." Her heart was shattered. An accident. A terrible life-taking accident.

Key Points

- The sentiment "if only" means that you are not in control.
- "If only" leaves you powerless.
- You must decide to leave regrets behind.

Moving Forward

Deal with reality rather than what might have been or what you think should have been.

"Things Could Always Be Worse" and Other Useless Wisdom

Being a person of faith, I believe the words written in scripture, but I can tell you from experience that there are words in scripture that are not helpful to a person in grief! In the appendix of this book I have included a more exhaustive list of things to say/not to say and to do/not to do. One of the things was not to quote scripture! (I realize that I have already broken that edict in this book! Please forgive me.)

He's in a better place. I thought if one more person told me that my husband was in a better place, I might throttle them! I didn't want him to be in a better place! I wanted him to be here with me! Selfish? Absolutely! Real and true? Absolutely! Do my beliefs tell me that being in heaven is better than being on this earth? Yes, and I do believe that, but in moments of grief we are usually only thinking of ourselves.

Perhaps we have never experienced this sort of pain—the pain of someone we loved being jerked out of our lives. Beliefs and emotional responses are oftentimes diametrically opposed during moments of grief. Be gentle. Realize that the grieving persons are not in a place to be analytical or logical. Think about it: It does not matter at all what a newly grieving person is saying or thinking! In time the fog of grief will lift, and most people will see things more clearly,

All things work together for good. It was two years before I was able to deal with the verse (Romans 8:28) that says, "all things work together for good to those who love God." I kept trying to decide how John's death was going to work for good in my life. How could that be? How could I ever say to myself that I was better off now? Finally, I decided that God said it and I believed it, and it was not necessary for me to interpret and nor to look into the future and discover that good for myself. Doesn't work that way!

Count it all joy. Yes, that is straight from scripture, but at the time of death, I could not even begin to count it all joy. This is certainly not the context of the verse. I know there is a deeper meaning to that verse, and I know that somehow it applies to me too. But I cannot think that any of us are supposed to find joy in death. That seems antithetical to me! I have heard many people be glad their loved one was no longer in pain. I understand that sentiment, but I don't think it is what we are talking about here.

You will see him again. Perfect. Unfortunately, I know enough from scripture to know that when I see him again in heaven, he will not be my husband. I wanted what I have now, not some new, improved relationship that is a non-relationship! In the years that have passed I now understand that when I too am in heaven, I will not desire marriage. Marriage is an institution for this current world. I must say that I did not find it comforting at all to be told that I would see just him again!

I know how you feel. Do you really? No, unless you have lost a spouse, you do not know how I feel. Watching your grieving mother or father after the loss of a spouse doesn't compare to experiencing the death of your own spouse.

He was old and you had a lot of years together.
At the time of death, most of us are not feeling particularly generous. We are a bit selfish. I don't care
how old he was. I still loved him. We still had a great
life. I try to never ask the age of one who has died.
Regardless the age, we will still miss our loved one.
Death is final.

People who are not married still suffer when they
lose a partner. Perhaps they have not been together
for thirty years, but maybe they were anticipating
being together thirty years. Engaged. Partnered but
unmarried. This is not time for judgment because you
don't agree with their living arrangement. This is the
time to reach beyond your own moral standards and
give love and acceptance to a grieving human. Don't
multiply their grief with judgments at this vulner-
able time.

Things could always be worse. Thanks, that is
really comforting. There will in fact always be something more horrific and more tragic than our own circumstances. Can you see how that is not comforting?

It is true. Things could always be worse, but to say
that is to deny the pain you are currently experiencing! If my garage burns down, destroying my car,
some would say things could have been worse. Yes,
they could. My house could have also burned to the
ground. My dog could have died in the fire. I could
have lost every bit of memorabilia that I possessed

for the past six decades and I could have had a safe that contained a million dollars and $100,000 worth of jewelry (I wish). Does that make you feel better? No, of course not! Things are bad enough without denying their enormity or comparing them to something worse you saw in the news! Now, find a place to find hope.

I say that because of an event from when my daughter was nine years old. She was struck by a car and in the hospital for seventy-five days. A poster on a door down the hall said, "Smile—things could be worse." Upon entering the room, a poster on the inside of the door said, "So I did, and they were!" I have never forgotten that sign. Whenever I hear someone say, "things could be worse," I always silently say to myself, "So I did, and they were!" Irreverent? Yes, but I happen to see the humor in the difficult things of life.

The truth is that we never know how the story will end. We certainly cannot determine the end through the fog of heartache and grief. We don't need to compare our tragedy to that of others, not to maximize and not to minimize. Our path is unique. Our circumstances are unique. The result depends in no small part on how to choose to deal with the tribulations that life brings. We can be bitter and lose the victories of the future or we can live with the hope

God puts in our hearts and trust Him for an outcome that may prove to be surprising and glorious.

In his book *Servant Leadership*, Dave Kuhnert poses the theory that we can only control three things: who we trust, how we react, and our perspective. According to our choice of perspective, we can be empowered, or we can choose bitterness and defeat. It's encouraging to see that we can change the course of our life by simply choosing our perspective.

Now, I would like to interject here that these verses and thoughts may not minister to your heart at this time. If they don't, please don't walk away in anger and pain. Maybe these truths are for later in your journey. Maybe these are not truths that will ever minister to your heart at all. But, do not let the fact escape you that only you can choose a perspective for your own life.

Find humor in the same things you previously found humor in: Aunt Edna's funny hat or Uncle Jimmy telling the same story over and over so that now you know it word for word. There's even humor in the insensitive things other people say to us. Imperfect words said by imperfect people that were meant to comfort but miss the mark. I once found myself responding to a very insensitive remark said to me only five months after John's death. The remark was, "You think you have a corner on grief? Well, you don't. My father died six years ago, and I grieve his loss daily." There are so many things wrong with that expression that I don't know where to begin. I simply said, "Tell me about your father."

As adults we understand that most people do not say things to cause us pain. People make hurtful remarks because they have not faced what you are now facing. They do not intend to be thoughtless. Their remarks are meant to comfort, but often miss the mark. Be forgiving. Be ready to offer a more thought-out response whenever you are attempting to comfort someone. Unfortunately, now you know. There is no teacher quite as good as experience.

Paul and Randy's Story

Paul and Randy had been together twenty-eight years. They had built a business and a life together. They owned a home together, took trips together and had dreams for the future. Paul was the business manager and kept a tight rein on Randy. Randy was the creative one. They owned a showroom in a decorative center that sold to businesses. They made me laugh and they helped me make money by giving me tips on what sorts of things were selling. Their showroom was exquisite and friendly. I loved to go there at the end of a hard workday of showing my goods in another showroom of the center. They had a way. A way of making the tired go away. I loved them both.

Randy could only be described as a goof! He always had fun. He made life fun! I was shocked when I went in one day to find that neither one of them was there. Gone on a doctor's appointment. Strange. Right in the middle of a market. I was anxious to call later and get an answer. I knew that Randy's mother had been ill and was afraid that she had taken a turn for the worse.

No, it was much more shocking than that. Randy was ill. Very ill. He had pancreatic cancer and his days were limited. Maybe two months. It was shocking information. Randy, so full of life. But isn't that always how it is? Seems like so many delightful and loveable folks go early.

Randy lived less than two months, and during that time he was horribly ill. So, as is often said, it was almost a relief when he passed quickly. Almost. We don't want our loved ones to be in agony, but we aren't ready for them to disappear from our lives either. Paul grieved. One day when I went in to visit, he told me of all the thoughtless things that had been said about Randy's passing. The dismissive remarks. The judgments. His heart was further damaged by these statements meant to help him see the error of his ways. There may never be a right time to approach these matters, but this is the worst time. Restrain yourself. Think of the compassion you would desire if you were in that place. Literally, walk in Paul's shoes for a while.

Key Points

1. People will make thoughtless comments.
2. Some common tenants of your faith may be difficult to accept now.
3. Forgive and move on.

Moving Forward

If there is someone in your life who is prone to judgment, avoid them if you can. If they still get the opportunity to speak hurt to you, forgive them. Words that are spoken thoughtlessly are meant to be forgiven. Don't focus on the hurtful words spoken. Focus on the positive.

More Shocking
for Sure

I have said many times not to compare your circumstances to those of someone else. Now, I'm going to say something new. I do think that some things that happen in some lives are MORE SHOCKING than others. As I have recounted in some of the stories in this book, life changes in a moment.

I always smile when someone says that their life changed forever in a moment. The fact is that is always the way change occurs! One moment you are single and the next you are married. One moment you are an undergraduate, the next you are a graduate. See my point? However, when the "thing" precipitating the change is negative—like a death—the result is much more surprising and much harder to process.

In the widow's support group that I facilitate, three women had lost their husbands in a moment. One in a tragic accident, and the other two in illnesses that occurred in a nanosecond. The first I discussed in an earlier chapter of this book. One of the others received a call saying that James was lying in the front yard. Yes, he had a widow-maker heart attack. That's what they call a heart attack where there is no warning and it takes your life immediately. The other sweet lady took her husband to the emergency room because he was suffering from abdominal pain. He was an especially large man, six-foot-four, so he went by ambulance. Upon arrival he was diagnosed with a perforated colon and rushed to surgery. He died at 2:30 a.m. Neither woman had time to prepare, practically or emotionally.

Do I think that their pain was deeper than my pain? No, I really don't and besides, we have already discussed not to compare! Forgive me while I do that! I think there is something very shocking about an expected death—something that takes our breath away—our breath coming in gasps the same as our loved one has gasped their last breath.

In her book *Option B*, Sheryl Sandburg says, "A traumatic experience is a seismic event that shakes our belief in a just world, robbing us of the sense that life is controllable, predictable, and meaningful." I think that is a fair description. An earthquake that leaves a chasm so wide and large that you feel as if the gap can never be closed again. The feeling that there is actually a hole in your chest, and you can feel the cold air whistling through the opening. Yes, I do believe that the unpredicted death must be shockingly hard to absorb.

I personally know only one person who has lost a loved one to homicide. I cannot begin to describe the hopelessness and helplessness that she felt in the face of those circumstances. Intense anger is also a predictable response. An anger deeper and that lasts longer than in a typical loss. And, if the person responsible is not found, those feelings may last much, much longer.

Suicide is another instance where I think many of the rules do not pertain to the rest of us. The helplessness of knowing that your beloved has lost his/her will to live is shocking. Suicide is one of the worst things that could occur in the lives of those left behind. These people deserve our special love, and we need to acknowledge our inability to understand. For the most part we can only listen and offer any service that helps them through this dark hour.

Suicide is a burden that I feel survivors take to their grave with them. I have heard many stories of elderly who still label themselves as "my mother or my father took his/her own life." A sad label forty or fifty years later.

If you know someone who has lived through either murder or suicide, he or she needs to seek professional counseling. And, further, the person needs to interview and be certain that the counselor is trained not only in grief, but the specifics of these horrifying circumstances. There are many support or bereavement groups specifically for suicide survivors and for survivors of murder. As a friend, you would be helping if you could find and research those groups.

All the potentials for service still apply to these folks. Listening and hugs are always welcome.

If There's Anything I Can Do

How many times have you said those words to a grieving person as you stood to leave after a wake, a viewing, a visitation, or a funeral service? Did you mean it? Of course, you did! I meant it each time that I said it! However, as we have already discussed, asking a grieving person (who thinks they are losing their mind) to project their needs into the future—even the next day, hour, or conversation—is impossible.

Some time ago, a young friend and I gave a talk about grief for a ladies' meeting at our church. We brainstormed several times before we decided what our focus would be. She had lost a two-year-old child, a tragedy of epic proportions. My husband had died, which I also consider a tragedy. We wanted to give helpful information rather than just garner sympathy. So, as I began, I said, "We could make you cry, but we're going to try not to!" Our focus was on what to say/what not to say. What to do/what not to do. Our talk was very well received because everyone wants to know how to comfort someone in the throes of grief. We want to say that perfect comforting phrase and walk away feeling better about ourselves.

Sorry. That is not going to happen. I am going to share with you some of what we shared in our talk that day. (In the index of this book, you will find a more complete section of things to do/not do.) First, these are not comprehensive. Let your imagination go from here. Use these suggestions and expand them. Make them more creative; go further with them. Secondly, we have all said the things on the list of phrases NOT to say! Yes, I have even said them once or twice since my husband's death! Don't condemn yourselves, or others, for trying and for saying the wrong thing! Determine to do better next time!

Let me preface these suggestions by reminding you of a few facts about grief. Grief is the natural response to a loved one being ripped from your life—whether expected or unexpected. There is no road map to grief, so don't look at how you or anyone else is walking through grief and make judgments such as "You need to get on with life." "It's time to begin living again," etc. Grief has a beginning, but there is no finish line because it is not a race or a contest. Grief takes as long as it takes for any single individual. The process is affected by the relationship; the state of things at death; regrets; and many more factors. We should never sit in judgment when we are not privy to all the details of the situation.

Let's go back to "If there is anything I can do, call me." Don't put the onus on the grieving to contact you. You contact them. "I'm off to the grocery. Can I pick up milk, bread, chocolate, wine?" That is helpful beyond measure because at the beginning of grief, many do not enjoy leaving the house. The home is ridiculously lonely, but then again, it feels safe there. Plus, my recollection is that I felt he (my deceased husband) was more there than anywhere. (I did realize he was not there!) An offer to pick up things from the grocery store is easy to accept! Helpful!

If you happen to run into a person out in public who has recently had a death, please do not begin a conversation about grief! That person may be attempting to get through the checkout line before bursting into tears. Don't ignore the situation completely (elephant in the room syndrome). Simply say something like, "You have been on my mind." "I'm thinking of you." "Can I call so we can get together?" These statements convey compassion without cornering the person like a wounded animal!

A comment that I've heard multiple times, often said to the parent whose child had died, is "God needed him/her in heaven!" Oh, horse feathers! Where does the idea originate that says the Creator of the universe, who blew the stars into the sky and named them all, decided that He needs the services of a three-year-old to assist in running heaven! Think before you say anything.

There is a myriad of things on the what-not-to-do list. Let's begin with: Don't stay away because you don't know what to say! Our loved one has already abandoned us. Don't abandon us too! If you spoke with someone daily, or weekly, still do that. Learn to let them speak. Their grief is natural. It is not about you. You do not have to carry their grief, nor do you have to relieve it. Walk through their grief with them. Again, when you encounter a person you know to be grieving, don't ignore the subject because it makes you anxious. Ask how they are doing today. Or, say "This is such a hard time for you."

My favorite way to address the grieving is to ask them a question. The question is always one that can be answered either yes or no or essay. This option gives the grieving person the opportunity to respond with a one-word answer or to respond with details. Such a question would be something like, "This season of the year (holidays, summer, Father's Day, etc.) must remind you so much of him (her). The response can then be a simple yes or no, or more often can be: "Yes, he loved the summer. We loved to go to the lake. He would fish and come home and bring dinner and we would have friends join us, sitting under the stars." And on and on. You have given the grieving person an opportunity to talk about their beloved, which addresses another important point. Please talk about the deceased!

I know that it is difficult, and many times I have heard people say that they don't want to bring up the subject because it may make the person cry. Well, yes, that is a possibility, even probability. However, they are crying sometime, somewhere. Everything makes them cry! They may as well be crying when relating a sweet story to someone who loves them and loved their loved one!

Give the grieving the opportunity to talk about their loved one! When no one speaks of them, the grieving may feel as if no one loved the deceased but them! Almost as if they were not important to anyone else. We know that is not true. Share their grief! Say the name. Relay an anecdote that you remember. It doesn't even have to be flattering; it needs to be kind! Simply calling the name when saying, "I know you miss Ray" is comforting. The absence of someone's name is a hurtful part of grieving. When we speak to our friends, we talk about our loved one calling him by name. Our loved one has disappeared from our life and now it seems that his name has disappeared too!

Another thing to avoid is personalizing. This conversation is NOT about you. Do not begin a story with, "My uncle Bob had this same disease, but he got giant sores all over his body, his hair all fell out, and they had to amputate all his limbs." Does that seem helpful to you?

Do not compare. Don't maximize or minimize. Don't say, "Losing an aunt is not nearly as difficult as losing a best friend." Their aunt could have been their best friend! And, yes, it could always have been worse. The entire family and all their friends and acquaintances could have been in the North Tower for a birthday party during 9/11! Yes, but do we have to go there? At the moment, the grieving person is doing all they can do to hold it together if their loved one died a natural, expected death. They are still gone!

Please do not compare death to divorce. I would never diminish the pain of divorce, but there is one huge difference between the two—death is final. When someone dies, there will never be a lunch where you sit down and reconcile your hurt and walk away satisfied or unsatisfied! THERE WILL NEVER BE THAT LUNCH. Death is final. No reconciliation is possible. No one ever chooses death. (Let's clarify and say, few choose death.) Someone chose divorce, even if it was not you. So, please do not compare death and divorce.

For the spiritual, please do not use this time to pass along your own theology or verses from scripture; they feel like an assault when delivered by a person who is trying to escape or make sense of the current pain and loss. And, since you have no idea what the person is feeling at this moment, scripture that is comforting to you may feel judgmental to them. They may desire the joy of the Lord, but they may be feeling bitter or angry at this exact moment. It is not your job to transfer them from anger to healing! In his book *Love Does*, Bob Goff says, "I don't think verses were meant to be thrown like grenades at each other. They were meant for us to use to point each other toward love and grace and invite us into something much bigger." So, be gentle. You have no idea what is behind the smile of your suffering friend.

One thing that is often said is "He's not suffering anymore." Yes, that is true, and I think it is okay for members of the family to express that sentiment. However, a declaration of that kind might be a step too far. The family member may be thinking that they would do anything to have the deceased back again. Listen more than you speak. Take your cues from the one in grief.

There are many stumbling blocks to overcome when we are attempting to comfort the grieving. To the best of our ability we should assess the situation prior to meeting with the grieving person. According to your relationship you are free to grieve with the person or else hold your own grief for later and comfort with your words or actions. Sometimes the grieving person will be comforted by us sharing our grief. At other times we allow the grieving person the space to express their grief without feeling that they need to comfort us! We must attempt to hold our feelings somewhat in check. Loud, emotional sobs might not be comforting. At times that would be exactly appropriate, but again, assess the situation prior to going to the venue.

And, as I stated earlier, choose your words prior to going, and also choose that one thing that you can do repetitively so that you are not at a loss of what to do. That may not always be possible, but when you can choose something you have done before, it keeps you from spending inordinate amounts of time deciding what to do.

We have talked about the what-not-to-dos. Let's talk about what you *can* do. Do something practical. Write a note or send a text. This allows the grieving person to read it at a time chosen by them. If the note comforts, they can save it and read it again. Take food, but not too much. Don't overwhelm the family with food that they will have to take care of at the end of the day. If the widow lives alone, simply make an extra portion and take it to them—this can go on for several months or weekly or semi-weekly or whatever your schedule allows. If your gift is organization, offer to be the food coordinator during the time family prepares and attends the funeral.

There are so many other things. Think of what YOU would need in the same situation. Dog sit. Pick up mail and papers if the grieving family is leaving town for a service. Take the laundry home and return it fresh and folded. Drive carpool. One of the most wonderful gestures was a friend who came by and took my car. He returned it full of gas, oil changed, and shiny clean. It was such a sweet gift!

DO call before you go by. DO share your favorite books. After some time goes by, DO ask the person to attend a social event, go to a bunko party, dinner, a concert. After a couple of months, most people go on with their own lives. Unfortunately, a new widow/widower is attempting to begin a new life! Don't forget them.

One of the things you might consider is to plan in advance what you are going to say and/or do. If you adopt some kindness that you like—as my friend did with taking my car to be serviced—do it every time. Then you don't have to question what you might do. Find something practical that is broad based and let it be your "thing." And, before you go to the home, visitation, wake, or funeral of the deceased, decide what you are going to say! Remember, the less you say the better, but plan to say something! Advance planning \allows you to forego platitudes that we often use when we are at a loss for the perfect thing to say.

Honor the relationship you had with the surviving spouse. The number of people who still remember to call me on the anniversary of his death has dwindled, but I am warmed by those who still remember. It is nice when one of his friends calls to say that he still misses him. It's also important not to change the relationship you once had with the widow/widower. Talk to them as frequently as you once did. If you once had lunch weekly, continue to do so. They will notice and feel abandoned if you change. They need you now! They need to feel something remains unchanged in their life!

Finally, give a lot of grace to the one grieving. They could be angry, in denial, crying all day under the covers, or even inappropriately talkative. Remember that you will walk this walk someday. We all will do it, probably more than once.

The Bible says in Matthew 5:4, "Blessed are those who mourn, for they will be comforted." Be a part of that comfort. You will be blessed and so will the one mourning.

Jimmy's Story

Jimmy's story is not uncommon to what happens to many men. Men don't generally seem to be equipped to face grief. Loneliness is even more overwhelming to the male gender. I would say that can be true of women also, but men tend to solve it quickly by replacing their mate as soon as possible. Jimmy lost his beloved wife, Deborah, after twenty-five years of marriage. She went from good health to death in only a week!

Jimmy had no time to prepare for an event so unwelcome and unexpected. In one month, he was on the dating sites. In ten months, he was remarried. The problem is he still had not grieved. His only grief experience was loneliness. True, loneliness is a huge and ongoing problem, but only a part of the grief experience. Jimmy found himself in a new marriage instead of grieving. He found anger always on the edge of his tongue. Jimmy didn't understand because he was not normally an angry person. Much time was spent repenting and apologizing. The story does not yet have an ending. Will his new wife endure, or will she give up on the relationship? Being that she is also a widow, she may realize that Jimmy skipped a necessary part of healing.

Walking through the process is the best answer. Don't drag another person into your pain. Be whole and healed prior to beginning something new. Your new relationship will have a much better chance of survival if you begin with the new you rather than the hurting you.

Key Points

1. Don't forego saying anything because you don't know what to say.
2. Do something.
3. Honor the relationship you had with the deceased and with the ones still living.

Moving Forward

Be forgiving for the inappropriate or unhelpful things that are said. Most often people are trying to be helpful and don't know how. Be generous of spirit.

Dream
a New Dream

I worked hard to overcome grief. I read books, attended seminars, and took good physical care of myself—exercising, eating well. I spent time with friends who love me. I read my Bible and carried a scripture with me daily to get through the tough moments. I did the work. AND I SLEPT. My body and soul were exhausted from seven years of caregiving and seven years of denying the fear and pain. Seven years of being the hero. The changes were slow, but the fog lifted.

And then, one day as I drove through the mountains of Colorado, something happened. The air was fresh and clean as I drove with my windows down through roller coaster-like mountain passes, with the road reaching toward the sky and then plunging to the depths near the gurgling stream. The hairpin curves were frustrating but were also the saving grace—making the heights and depths both doable. Tiny wildflowers sprang up, showing hope and resilience from the long, cold winter. They danced through the solid granite, an advertisement for survival of the fittest! I breathed in the beauty of the mountains as if I had never seen them before. I hadn't really seen them through these new eyes.

I felt as if I had pulled over and took off the suit of armor that I had worn to protect myself from further pain. The heaviness of grief lifted, and I felt the joy of life pulsing through my veins. You see, grief is for a time. Life is big. And I was shocked to ask myself, *what if the best of life is yet to be!*

My friends said that I had a glow—the same thing that was said to me immediately after John's death. At that time, it had to do with the euphoria of a caregiver who had completed her assignment. Sadly, the euphoria was always short-lived and followed by an emotional crash into tears when the reality of my loss came back into focus. And guilt. Now, it has to do with healing and hope and hunger for a new life. And occasionally a little guilt. In her book *Option B*, Sheryl Sandburg wrote, "More than half the people who experience a traumatic event report at least one positive change." There comes a time to discover that positive change.

For some reading this book you are not even close to healing. For some, you have grieved and are ready to move into the next phase. It is easy to hit a wall. Even though you are mentally ready to go forward, for an extended time you have been in a place of grieving. Grieving is often done in near isolation. You are now ready to break out of that place of isolation. Problem is, now you truly are making a new life. How do you do this?

In David Kuhnert's book, Servant Leadership, he details a method for analyzing how to attain our goals. He calls the method Here/There/Path. First identify where you are beginning. This is your "here." Next. identify your goal. This is your "there." Finally determine a path you will use to achieve your goal. Those of us in grief have fully acknowledged our "here." Our "there" is to be healed, productive, contributing to society as before. The last piece of the puzzle is the "path." In many ways, the path is the most difficult part. The life we had before with our spouse took many years to develop. It began on a high note—a new marriage. This new beginning will be from a harder place—grief, loss, sadness. Devastation. The thing to recognize is that if you have worked hard to heal from your loss, you can now make the decision to go forward with your life. Previously we talked about perspective. You must be empowered to go forward. To choose to accept the healing that you have been working toward.

I really like John Piper's advice for the grieving. Reverend Piper is a valued octogenarian theologian with much wisdom. He says, "Occasionally, weep deeply over the life that you hoped would be. Grieve the losses. Feel the pain. Then wash your face, trust God, and embrace the life He has given you." He goes on to say, "No. You will not define me, sorrow. Yes, let there be weeping in those seasons—feel the losses. Then wash your face, trust God, and embrace the life He's given you."

I think that what Reverend Piper is saying is simply a rewording of the words we have all heard from scripture—even those who are not at all spiritual have heard these words!

ECCLESIASTES 3:1-4

To everything there is a season,
A time for every purpose under heaven:
A time to be born,
And a time to die;
A time to plant,
And a time to pluck what is planted;
A time to kill,
And a time to heal;
A time to break down,

And a time to build up;
A time to weep,
And a time to laugh;
A time to mourn,
And a time to dance.

These words, those of Reverend Piper, and the ancient words from scripture point to the fact that grieving is real. We must set aside a time in our life to actively grieve our loss. But grief is not our life. We all have a purpose in our life. We will all have loss in our life. Work to both embrace that loss and to embrace life with the new dimension—the you that continues to live after loss. Find your purpose, even though it may now be different than it was before. Engage life, with all its thorns, and see the possibilities.

The most helpful advice I was given was to take up a new hobby. The reason is that it would be an activity that you have never done with your spouse, and therefore, you will not miss his presence in the doing of the new activity. I took up photography. I love to capture the art of God! I have hung pictures taken since 2013 throughout my home. Another benefit is that my home is a little different now—more mine rather than ours.

I like that I took up something creative, so that I can observe and enjoy it hanging on my walls. You may not be interested in photography. How about cooking classes? (Your friends will love you!) Dance classes. Adult education classes. Take up a sport: hiking or cycling. Take art lessons. Learn meditation. Go back and get a new advanced degree!

Now, the next step. For me the next step was to take classes to hone my craft. For you, perhaps you could give a class on something. Maybe join a book club or a discussion group through a local university.

Next, begin a social life again. I made it my policy to always accept invitations from friends. Go out to dinner. Go to plays. Attend sporting events with your friends—for their children and grandchildren. Buy tickets and share one with a friend. Take a friend.

Serve others. Serving others helps you to find gratitude again. Gratitude brings healing as you focus on others more than yourself. As you change your self-focus, you will again see the needs of others. Volunteer at Meals on Wheels or become a pink lady at your local hospital. Some hospitals need volunteers in the NICU to hold newborn babies! Volunteer at the nursery at church. Take food to a shut-in or bake cookies for neighborhood children. Join the neighborhood watch. There are many, many organizations that can use your expertise—libraries, schools, hospitals, and more. Your service will serve to get you out of your home—out of isolation.

For some time, your full attention has been focused on your own pain. As you heal you will need to replace those times of self-reflection with activities that refine you as more than a widow. Your energy will return as you become rested from the exhausting journey of grief. You must find ways to channel your returned energy. Be thoughtful. Try to learn the word "no." You will become a target for those seeking new volunteers. Pace yourself. Pursue new endeavors. Try new things.

Dating. Dreaming a new dream would not be complete without addressing dating. My best advice is to not begin dating until you are certain that your heart has healed. This is important for the obvious reason—don't give your heart away before it fully belongs to you again, and it is only fair to begin any relationship from a place of honesty and integrity. You don't want to go out to dinner and burst into tears for no apparent reason! And, further, what if this relationship has the potential to be longer term and you go into it still grieving and don't give it the appropriate chance? Dating too early will not heal your heart. Dating could potentially be a setback. You cannot serendipitously replace a great love. A great love is developed over time, slowly, deliberately. Rushing into a new relationship does not honor your grief nor assist your healing.

You must leave your regrets behind and reach forward to first know who you are now, and then to step into that role and embrace the new you—the

one with the new dimension—the person who has
stumbled through one of the most difficult parts of
life and survived. So, be bold, be brave, and be ready
to dream a new dream.

Key Points:

1. Grief is real. We will all do it in our life.
2. Do the hard work to recover. It's hard
   and necessary.
3. Begin a new dream. Find your purpose.

Moving Forward

*"Someday we'll find it, the rainbow connec-
tion, the lovers, the dreamers and me."*

—KERMIT THE FROG

GUIDE TO

———

CAREGIVING

Reflections on Caregiving

I have never thought of myself as a caregiver. Unfortunately, I am not the servant type. My beloved husband loved to serve. He served everyone—all the time. He loved to get you another cup of coffee, or another glass of iced tea, to pick up the dirty dishes, to turn down the bed at night. It was his way of showing love. I probably spent twenty years with him before I realized the best way to love him was to serve him! He understood that the best.

He loved a freshly vacuumed floor. We had a short-haired white dog who shed. He hated dog hair. In our last decade together, I would rush home in late afternoon from whatever I was involved in and vacuum the floor. I never made a big deal of it. Never spoke of it. Never patted myself on the back. He couldn't quite put his finger on it either, but would remark, "Things really look nice." I would smile. I had learned to serve him.

It was different to be a caregiver than to serve because no one desires to become a caregiver. For the most part caregiving is a role that is thrust upon us— maybe for financial reasons or maybe for love, as with me. I freely admit that in the beginning I resented some of the things I was doing that he had previously done. I also resented not being able to travel and the sound of that darned oxygen machine. That sound was the elevator music of my life—for seven years. Initially, it wore on my nerves. I longed for the serenity of silence.

As John's illness progressed, he was home more and more. His only day away from home for any significant time was Tuesday. On that day he had an executive meeting that took him away for hours. Tuesday became my day to stay at home. I had always treasured the sanctity of my home—alone! Now, it was truly a treasure. I rarely ever had outside-the-home commitments on Tuesday. I cherished those days of quiet.

Time marched on and things changed. God was gracious to me. The changes were slow. Emphysema is a slow-moving condition. As things progressed, two things happened. The first was that my duties were multiplied—there were more and more things that John could not do. And second, the resentment died away. I will never feel that I stepped into the role of servanthood with the same relish that John enjoyed. I can honestly relate that now I can hardly recall what I was going through—because what he was going through was very difficult to witness.

C. S. Lewis said, "It takes courage to live through suffering; and it takes honesty to observe it." John had the courage. I learned to face our circumstances with honesty. I attempted not to "go ahead." I tried not to imagine how devastating it would be to live without him. (Occasionally, I would land in self-pity and wallow there for a time.) Mostly, I took my cues from the courage I was witnessing. The fact is, I had no idea what was rushing at me. I attempted to live each day as it came. In doing so, I was able to piggyback on John's courage.

I recall an incident from four years before John died. We sat on our back patio watching the golfers. John had been in the hospital and only home for a few days and was quite discouraged that he had not risen to his previous level of health. This was probably three years into his illness. We were quietly sitting in our rocking chairs hearing the golfers laughing and cursing as they hit a bad shot. Suddenly, John said, "I pray at night not to wake the next day." I still recall that day vividly. My heart took a hiatus from beating as I considered my next words. Having been a chaplain for a number of years, I knew that it was important that I allow him to talk about death. The dying wants even NEED, to talk about death. Finally, I said, "I think I can understand that. It is hard for me to hear, but I think I understand it." A floodgate was opened. We sat there and talked about death. Dying. What was next. John had never inquired from the doctors about his prognosis or how long he had left to live. Now, in a moment, the elephant had left the room.

We turned a corner that day. John wanted to give me information that I would need when he was no longer in this world. I wanted him to give it. I needed to hear what he thought I should do—sell the house or keep it, move to be closer to the children or stay near my friends. So many things. Many women do not get the luxury of hearing those things. When a husband is taken in a heartbeat, through accident or heart attack or something even worse, there is no time to put things in order. We got to discuss all the fine details of his instructions for me.

I also knew, with great finality, that I had the luxury of seeking other advice, but I had relied on him for three decades. I trusted his wisdom. Yeats said, "If suffering brings wisdom, I would wish to be less wise." I wholly concur with that, but then death and suffering are not a choice we get to make! Certainly, none of us would choose either one!

I felt like those seven years were a gift to me. Now, as I watch other widows navigate other circumstances, I realize that in seven years we were able to accomplish a number of important things: get our affairs in order, make peace with any regrets we had, say all the things that needed to be said, walk through the journey together in a sweet, intimate way that a sudden death denies. Yes, those seven years were a gift.

I would like to share that gift with you. Although I did not have any formal training or instruction in caregiving and grieving, I learned a lot about both from on-the-job training. As I share a few of the things I learned along the way, my hope is that your path can be made a little easier.

Being an
Advocate

You have now added a new item to your job description, advocate. We all need an advocate. Someone who is dedicated to protecting us, making certain that we are safe, filling the potholes of life before we fall into them! A patient particularly needs an advocate.

I felt that John was blessed to have the health care that he received. His physicians were focused on the quality of his life rather than the quantity. Unfortunately, many doctors seem to be keeping score of some kind. When someone is ill and their systems are giving out, wearing out, quantity (the amount of time remaining) is probably not the first concern. Being comfortable and as pain-free as possible is a great place to be.

John's main health care was from several hundred miles away until the last year. He was no longer able to travel to them. So, they managed his care, his hospitalizations, medications, etc., by phone, text, and email. For his final hospitalization in our local hospital, there was a doctor who someone called in to consult. I did not call him. I also did not like him at all. He was extremely unhappy to be on the "B" team. (I think it was a billing thing. When we got his invoices weeks after going home, we found that he had charged $200 each time he came by and read the chart! At those times he didn't even enter the room.)

Upon discharge from the hospital he stood in the doorway from across a large room and told me to get John to his doctors immediately because he had lung cancer. He said it in a loud voice, loud enough for John to hear from the bathroom. In God's providence, John did not hear! A month later when he went to see the "A" team doctors for what turned out to be the last time, I relayed to his doctor what had been said. I had not told John because he could not have endured any aggressive treatment in his weakened state. His physician was shocked and looked over his records, carefully stating he could see no evidence of lung cancer. Instead of freaking out like I wanted to, I was a good advocate for John. I waited until the appropriate time. He would have been devastated to think that he had lung cancer to go along with his emphysema. He did not. My instincts were correct, and John was saved from undue worry and stress.

The point here is that not all physicians are going to be on board with what you have decided. If your emotions are inflamed, your path will be. Don't be deterred. You know how the patient wants to be treated. You were a part of those decisions. Don't take a new path now.

Another physician wanted to put John on a major blood thinner. When I refused, he stated that John would certainly have a stroke. I said that we would cross that bridge if we came to it. When I spoke with his personal doctor, he agreed. He saw no reason for blood thinner, and further, as John was now unsteady, he confirmed that John could bleed out from a mere fall without us even knowing until it was too late. I'm not suggesting that you substitute your own judgment for that of a qualified physician. I'm simply saying that it is good to know the facts and make a logical decision based on the facts. Or, get a second opinion!

Tests like PSAs and mammograms are probably not indicated for a person in end of life. Some doctors order them. Think about if your loved one could survive radical treatment like radiation and chemo before you allow those kinds of tests. Don't add another layer to the cake you are already baking!

The nurses at one facility wanted to clean their hands as they left the room. I wanted them to clean their hands *before* touching John. We went around and around. My feeling was that they were touching door handles (is anything worse?) between other rooms and his. A nursing supervisor was called in to explain the policy to me. I explained gently, yet firmly, that I wanted to see their hands be cleaned. John was fragile, and the smallest infection could be deadly. I won, but they were not happy for a couple of days. My feeling was that they would get over it and John was less likely to get an infection. Be a wise advocate.

Be an advocate with family too. Family can be demanding and thoughtless. Not usually, but you are probably spending untold hours each day/week with your patient. You KNOW how long he has been up, if he needs to rest. If they are toward the end of life (and this could be months), you also know how much stimulation is good for them and when it is time for visitors to go. If your home is usually quiet with just the sound of the television, small children or lots of visitors who are shouting or running can be too much stimulation. Those could be his favorite grandchildren whom he misses, but brief visits are better than long ones. Some family members live far away and can't come for frequent visits. Put them up with friends or in a hotel if possible. Then, they can come for an hour, go away, and return for another visit. Problem solved.

The hearing is the last sense to go. Please be careful what is said within earshot of the patient. His eyes may be closed. He may appear to be sleeping. Many years ago, my cousin was dying of a brain tumor. He was about thirty-eight years old at the time. On one of our visits, he had been comatose for several months. I was sitting in the room with his mother and we began talking about his children. We noticed that he had a few tears running down his face. His mother patted him and said that he always cried when anyone spoke of his children. Please, filter what you say and monitor the conversations of visitors. The patient may not be able to speak but may absolutely be able to hear!

A very touchy subject can be bringing hospice into the situation. Many patients object on the basis that you have given up on them. I am a huge fan of hospice. They spent nine beautiful months with us. The mission of hospice is to provide care for the patient and the family. The earlier they are brought into the equation, the better it is for everyone! The nurse who regularly provided care would come weekly and sit and visit with John. We looked forward to her visit. She was delightful. Because she came and stayed more than five minutes, we had time to ask questions and have good conversations that didn't end after a cursory examination.

Check into hospice early on. Educate yourself. You can introduce the idea of hospice from a different perspective if you have learned early on what the benefits are of hospice. Waiting until the end frightens the patient and, quite frankly, isn't as much assistance to the family. While hospice is particularly helpful in pain management and palliative care for the patient, the benefits to the caregiver and family might outweigh those benefits! Understanding symptoms is huge as health declines. It would be a daunting task to be waiting for answers from a physician each time something changed. Hospice also has physicians who are regular participants in the care of your loved one.

Being an advocate means anticipating the needs of the patient. Being an advocate means knowing the desires of the patient before final decisions need to be implemented. Being an advocate means being willing to be strong in the face of challenging decisions and downturns in the health of the patient.

Ready, Set, Go

I'm not certain that any of us really plan on being a caregiver. You may gradually find yourself in the role of caregiver or you may suddenly find yourself as a caregiver. Whether it is a role that comes about gradually or in a moment, it is a role that we are seldom prepared for. And, the job description often varies. Some will begin as full-time caregivers of patients with severe challenges. Some will serve a patient who has escalating needs. Either way, there are many things that intersect and will be helpful for whatever you are facing.

First of all, let me say that a sense of humor is the most important tool in your tool chest. If you haven't learned to laugh at yourself, now is an excellent time to begin. Some of the things you laugh at now would have been offensive or seemed insensitive or less than genteel at another time in your life. That was a different life. Hopefully, you and the patient have a relationship that will allow you to laugh at some of the awkward situations you will now be facing. BE CAREFUL not to laugh with others *about* the patient! Laugh *with* the patient. These will be private, intimate times between the two of you that help to erase some of the pain and awkwardness.

The longer you stay in denial about your current situation, the more likely your depression will grow. I am not recommending that you act in a Pollyanna way—as if your situation is different. What I am saying is that acceptance requires some grieving as you find a path to acceptance.

Earlier in the book I talked about the here/there path. Acceptance of your "here" is an important first step. Each of you who are reading will have to make that determination. Is this the beginning of the end of a life? Is this caregiving session just that, a session? A time after an accident or major surgery when the patient will hope to improve? This section is mainly written to the caregiver who is looking toward an ending that they anticipate, but do not want! Learn what you can laugh at with your patient! When something falls on the floor and makes a mess, it is better to laugh than to be angry!

I have a friend who has lost a great deal of her sight in the last couple of years. The beginning was devastating for her, her family, her friends. Losing your sight at an early age is difficult. Those were difficult days. We had to learn to speak our name when we walked into a group where she was talking so that she would know who had walked up. It was a slow process for her of grieving and fear for her future. I saw her last night and she made a joke about her perfect driving record over the past two years—of course, she is no longer driving! That is a perfect example of grieving a loss and then laughing at yourself at some point.

Initially, one of the most important aspects both for the patient and the caregiver is to be informed. Learn everything you can about the illness you are both facing. My one hesitation is that I found that I never wanted to ask certain questions of the doctor. I did ask the general questions, but in seven years I never asked the prognosis. I sometimes wondered where we were, but somehow, I felt that particular question was not mine to ask. The doctor doesn't really have an answer anyway. If the patient wants to know, let him ask. Talk with your patient about anything the person wishes to discuss. Don't put negative thoughts into his or her head that the person may not have addressed. Don't do it in the form of a question. Just don't do it. Let the person guide you. Be a sounding board and willing to discuss the hard things, but don't plant your own questions! It's not unlike talking to a four-year-old about sex. Let the person ask the questions. Don't give more information than you're asked but be prepared to reply. Be gentle and be thoughtful!

As time progresses, you will find that your loved one leans on you to run interference for him/her. Time will make this easier with almost no communication—a feeling, or a knowing, anticipation based on previous experience. One day my husband had visitors from out of town. They had come in to spend time with him. I was surprised to find that he seemed rather anxious to be alone with them. As the time for them to arrive approached, he asked if I would stay with them as they visited. I found that request surprising as the visitors were old friends. They had a wonderful time talking about old times, and the three of them all realized without it being said that this was the last time they would see one another. John insisted that I go to lunch with them. Without it being said, I knew that I was now his protector! He counted on me to tell a guest that it was time for them to go when he was tired. My presence gave him confidence. That's quite a special feeling for a caregiver!

Patience. Lord, give me patience, and give it to me now! Patience is a huge requirement in caregiving. Things that were once easy are now a huge challenge! Follow the directions of the doctors and therapist on what things the patient should do for themselves and what things they can turn over to you. I can only guess how depressing it must be not to be able to do all the things we all take for granted—getting to the bathroom, showering, getting in and out of bed. If the doctor wants the patient to continue doing those things, assist as little as possible. Be there but be in the background. Be alert but don't be superglue! And, learn to hold your tongue and not grab something and take over because you are in a hurry. The days of being in a hurry are behind you.

The golden rule applies now more than ever. Treat others as you would want to be treated yourself. Include the patient in conversations. If they are sitting, sit with them—don't stand over them and talk. That may not always be possible, but as much as is possible, stay at their level. Don't treat them as a child. They are not a child even though they may be unable to do many things they once did; i.e., putting on shoes and socks. Tying shoes. Buttoning buttons. Take the job and talk about something else as you do it. Changing the subject to the weather, the sports team, the kids helps the patient not to focus on what they cannot do! Don't answer for them even if you know the answer unless they want you to do so. Let the patient retain his dignity. It's important at a time when so much is being taken away. Be respectful.

Take your cues from the patient. If your patient is an optimistic person and doesn't show his fear, take your cues from him. Try to cry your most tears away from the patient. If the patient is experiencing the expected grief, grieve with him. Cry with him. Be real. Find ways to say what you want/need to say without being Debbie Downer.

I had phrases that I used to encourage John. He hated that I had to do everything for him, and I reminded him that he had served me all of our years together. I focused on the word *partner*. I said again and again that I thought we had made great partners. I wanted to take away the negative feelings of being helpless and reinforce the feeling that as a team we had faced many trials together. A team. A partnership. I was doing my part. I wanted the focus to be taken away from *helpless* and I wanted it to be subtle.

You will find that caregiving is a roller coaster ride and you never anticipate when you may go from things going well to a downward spiral that appears unstoppable. Other things to consider are family pictures and videos. Someone who was a professional photographer/friend came one day and brought her camera. She made wonderful photographs that I treasure. Admittedly, John looked frail, but he still looked great to me and I was glad to have current photos. Another idea is to get all the family or as many as possible together and make a video of the patient. Make it an interview. You probably already know all the important facts and fun stories of his life. All the better to get him to tell them one more time. You will treasure that video! You will find that hearing the voices of family in the background makes you smile and laugh as they join in the fun.

Many of us are hesitant to be the center of attention, and some of us are worse than others, but I find that if there are family or friends in the room to encourage and be a part of the fun, the patient or honoree will forget that they are in front of a camera. Relax. Enjoy, but this is a very important step. The entire family will treasure the sound of a voice once it has departed forever. You will never regret spending the energy to assemble this group. Make it fun for everyone!

Plan some things into each day that you can do together that you can both share and enjoy. Pictures from past vacations you have taken are excellent. Consider watching a movie that is a favorite and you previously saw together. The fact that you have seen it before means that it will be easier to follow when thinking is not as clear as it once was, or the patient is distracted by pain or discomfort. If the patient is up to it, play a card game that you once enjoyed. If your patient always read the paper and is not able to do so now, read to him. Or, read the Bible or a favorite book. Help your patient to feel plugged into the world so that he will not feel isolated.

And, there are all those irritating computer games we want our grandchildren to stop playing! You would be surprised how distracting it can be after you teach someone to play solitaire with whatever technology you have. I taught my husband to play and sometimes it nearly drove me crazy, but I realized that his mind was occupied when he was doing it. Distracted is a great plus for them, and you too!

Nature has an amazing way of calming both the patient and the caregiver. When the weather was agreeable, we often sat outside together in the rocking chairs overlooking the golf course. We watched the golfers and the birds and had casual conversations as we sat there together.

One of the most fun things we did, and I now regret that we only did it once, was to go for a ride. John did not want to go. He felt fragile and our home was the place he felt the safest. I understood, but I also felt strongly that a change of scenery would be beneficial to him. After much coaxing, I talked him into a ride. The thing that pushed him over the edge was the promise of stopping at a local drive-in hamburger joint for a cheeseburger and chocolate milkshake! He had not been out of the house in months and was delighted to see the changes that were happening in our town. Having been in construction, John loved seeing the new buildings. Yes, he was tired when we got home and needed a nap. Truth is that he would have had a nap anyway. He loved the trip!

One thing of continual pleasure for John was music. I downloaded music that I labeled "John's Music." Music that he loved. Music that gave him pleasure. As time marched on and John became more ill, I would play that music when he reclined in his chair. Often, I would think he was sleeping and then see his lips moving silently to the music. I loved it!

An extremely helpful thing when caring for a loved one at home is a baby monitor. Monitors are very sensitive, and having it meant that if John was asleep, we had the option to be in another room. As soon as he stirred, we would be there in his room. That small device gave us a small amount of comfort and freedom. It was great! Most of us know a young family who no longer uses their monitor and are pleased to share it with you for a time.

These are a few of the needs and concerns to address at the beginning of caregiving. In chapters to follow I will discuss a few of the practical things that should be addressed at the onset of caregiving such as making final plans for funeral services and assembling all necessary paperwork, both legal and practical, to facilitate assisting in final business and personal care decisions.

Persevering
for the
Caregiver

Learning the basics of physically handling the patient is imperative for a caregiver. These instructions can come from a nurse or someone professionally trained to work with patients. Hospice would be an excellent source, but there are many home care companies that could also provide this service. Any nominal fee that you incur would be preferable to injuring yourself! Simple procedures like moving a patient from the bed or to the chair to the bed is difficult if you do not know these basics.

Put together a list of your support system. These
include friends and family, including someone who
can be your 3 a.m. friend. This is a person who can be
called any time of day or night for emotional support.
As caregivers, we tend to do our heaviest worrying
in the middle of the night. For most of us our melt-
downs come in the deep of night. The darkness tends
to bring out the darkest doubts. Have someone you
can call. While I never placed that call, I had someone
who knew I might call during a meltdown. Let me
say that this person needs to be someone who can
respond well in crisis, emotional or medical. Many
times, it is better to have someone who does not
know the patient, thereby being your support rather
than that of the patient. The patient will have plenty
of supporters.

Part of your support system should consist of
friends of the patient who agree to make periodic
visits to help make the patient feel important in the
lives of others. You can also let these friends know
that if the patient seems down or blue you may call
upon them to help distract him and cheer him up.

Members of the clergy or whoever does home visits
from your local church or synagogue also need to be
alerted to the need for scheduled visits. Our church
was very gracious in this regard. I would notify the
elders whenever John was feeling down or worrying
about something. I would give them a call and several

would arrive. It felt very much like a party! They would sit with us and talk about interesting things before asking about what was going on. One or the other of us would communicate the issues of the day. They would give input and pray. When they left, we both felt better!

Once you have a support team, call upon them to relieve you occasionally. We all need a haircut now and then. It is nice to go out with friends for lunch. Or just run errands. Knowing that you can get a couple of hours on Thursday gives you something to look forward to. And, maybe you want to go to the park or to a movie.

Have something to keep your hands busy rather than just sitting. John watched entirely too much cable news for me. And, he wanted me to be with him. In October of his last year (he died on 12-12-12), I began needlepointing Christmas stockings for the grandchildren. I don't exactly enjoy needlepoint, but you cannot imagine what memories it brings back when I see those Christmas stockings hanging on the fireplace these six years later! I have great joy and satisfaction for those hours spent sitting with John in his year of life.

There are many less intense things to do with your hands. Some people read books or do crossword puzzles. Others draw, sketch, do Zen tangles, or perhaps even enjoy adult coloring books. Most any of those things help to occupy your mind.

One of the best and most important things you need to program into each day is a time for exercise. Something as easy as a short walk can work wonders for your mind and body. You might have to use a treadmill if you can't leave the patient, but make exercise part of your daily routine.

Whether or not you are an introvert or an extrovert, you should also add time in each day for quiet. Any way you use this time is appropriate. Prayer, meditation, or deep breathing exercise all count. Any of these will help you clear the tension from your shoulders and the fog from your brain.

Don't be a hero or a martyr. This could be a marathon rather than a sprint. And, please realize that the patient may become stressed if he sees you getting to the burnout stage. He doesn't need more to worry about. A smiling caregiver is preferred over a frowning, exhausted one!

Making
Final Plans

There are so many difficult decisions to face and talk about when facing the end of life. No one wants to say goodbye. No one wants to be the one to talk to the loved one who is dying. Someone must do the hard things. Often as a spouse we feel that we know the mind of our mate. Unfortunately, sometimes that is not the case. Clarify by talking about the hard things.

Begin the process of assembling both the legal and practical information that will be helpful when the patient is no longer able to do so because of declining health. The following chapters include suggestions for beginning this process.

An honest conversation with the patient about his/her desires about hospice or palliative care should be done long before the decision needs to be made. This allows the conversation to be less emotional for either the patient or the one assisting in making the decision when the time comes for palliative care. The patient may desire that every single option be exercised to keep them alive. Every single treatment attempted. Other patients will desire that extraordinary measures not be taken. You will need this information for the advance directives, but if these delicate things are addressed early, the decisions will be made before they become quite so emotional.

One of the things about hospice care is that most people wait too late to call them into service. The earlier that hospice is called, the more help they will be to the family. And, the earlier that you have the conversation and get it out of the way, the less anxious the patient will be when it is finally time to call. A friend related that her husband asked hospice when they arrived, "Are you going to kill me?" He said it jokingly, but it is probably one of the biggest fears of a lot of patients.

A pertinent question is whether the patient desires to die at home or in the hospital. That is a very intimate question that you should decide jointly. My husband feared that if he died at home that I would have difficulty with that later. I expressed my wish for him to be at home because sitting in a hospital for weeks is a really difficult thing to do. As time goes on, you will fear leaving them even though they may be receiving excellent care. If they are in the hospital, the fear is that the patient will die when you go home to take a shower, maybe the only time you have been away for days! That is one of the reasons to die at home, the comfort of the family. However, the decision must be made jointly. Perhaps you would not want to sleep in the room where your spouse died! I find it somewhat comforting.

Are there people whom the patient wants to see or doesn't desire to see? There was someone whom my husband did not want to see. I persuaded him to see that person. I felt that it would be generous of him to see them even if he didn't want to do so. I promised to monitor and not let the visitor overstay.

Are there memories and stories that the patient would like to record for posterity? That should be done early in the process before the patient is unable to be comfortable.

What are their desires for a funeral? Do you own a burial plot, or do they want to be cremated? If cremation, would they like their remains to be spread? Would they like the service to be in a church or other place? Many people have a reception at their favorite place or their favorite club.

At the appropriate time the caregiver, or the nearest relative of the patient, should sit down and talk with the beloved patient about his/her final wishes. I would guess that many of us living with a spouse might be surprised at some of their expressed wishes. Make a checklist and make the visit informal but give the conversation the sense of importance it deserves. "I would really like to know your feelings on a final funeral service. I understand that you will not be there, but we would like to honor your wishes." Begin without emotion or fanfare but begin! If you are a spouse, you could both put your wishes onto paper at the same time. Perhaps that would be less threatening. We all know that we could be struck by a bus while taking out the trash.

If clergy will be conducting the service, have them come and visit and talk with the patient about his desires. My husband planned his entire service from the speakers to the music. It was a joyous celebration of life. For a year afterward, people related how memorable the service was and how meaningful it was too. You can always add your favorite song later!

Make a list of questions you need answers to and bring it with you. (I have included a basic list of questions to get you started.) Record the information and put it in a place with other important documents. Some people make all the funeral arrangements and pay for them prior to the death of the patient. This is fine, but I don't think you should tell the patient. You never want to give the patient the feeling that you are standing around waiting for them to take their final breath.

My husband wrote his obituary four years prior to his death. I can remember a member of the family who died quite suddenly. It was extremely difficult to compile the obituary. The day that John gave me his obituary to type, I cried all day as I typed. I knew then how glad I was that I would not be saddled with this task at the time of his death! I really would have been a mess! Plus, with all the emotion of death, we might fail to include something extremely important.

John and I did not attend church for several months prior to his death. We had a constant trail of visitors, but we were not in church as such. In July prior to his death in December, a friend called and asked if they could set up a little party for some of our closest church friends to come and say hello/goodbye. They desired to do it far enough prior to his death for him to enjoy it himself. About eighty people came. They brought food, napkins, everything needed for a party. When they left, they took everything with them and took out the trash! The only thing they left was good memories!

We also had a final party. It was a spontaneous party about a week prior to death. On a Tuesday evening people just began showing up. I kept the front door unlocked all during this three-week period of time because it kept my dog from barking! People felt free to come in without ringing the bell, which made the dog bark. Thirteen people were in his room before it was finished, including two of the people who would sing and play guitar at his service. We sang the songs that would be sung at his service. He somehow found the breath to sing along and kept asking for one more song. John took that opportunity to give sweet encouragement to a couple he dearly loved. Everyone still talks about that one last party, and I am positive John still tells the story in heaven. The evening was joyous! Memorable! And fun! I highly recommend it.

Those last three weeks of life were extremely difficult. I was more exhausted when it was over than I have ever been before, and I hope that I never feel that way again. However, I would like to stress that those hours, days, and weeks were some of the sweetest of our marriage. Conversations were honest and real. John made some funny observations about the dying process and we spent time just being together. It is stressful to watch your loved one die. It is also physically exhausting. We were turning him every two hours, so we were getting little sleep. Even then, I still feel that time to be priceless.

The last thing I would like to add is that your experience might not be like my experience. John was unable to breathe and that causes great anxiety. If your loved one is in horrific pain, I can imagine that your experience might be totally different. I would not want to create any extra stress by giving you expectations that might not come to fruition.

Make your patient as comfortable as possible. Be patient. Be gentle. Be kind. Treat them as you would want to be treated. Give them encouragement and answer questions honestly. Satisfy their desires as much as possible. This is your last service to them. And, my hope for you is a sweet, gentle passing.

Suggestions for Final Preparations

- Go over where you are going to put all the final documents for safe storage. This will make the patient feel as if he/she still has some part in planning.
- Ask for the desires and wishes of the patient on hospice care or palliative care.
- Where does the patient want to die—at home or in the hospital?
- Are there people the patient does/does not want to see in these final days?
- Where would the patient like to be buried, or if cremated, where should his ashes be placed?
- Who should speak besides clergy?

- Flowers, or donations to charity? If a charity, what charity?
- Select the music to be played at the service.
- Write the obituary and determine where it should appear.

Common Fears of the Dying

Fears of the dying process:

"What will I feel?"

We can certainly understand this fear because none of us have died! The only things written about this comes from the perspective of those who say they have "died and come back." According to your own theology this may or may not comfort you. Of course, the patient is concerned. We are all concerned about the unknown. Talk with clergy, chaplains, and hospice workers in advance so that you will have an answer prepared at the time of the question.

"I don't want to be a burden."

My husband expressed this concern. I reminded him how he had served me all his life and it was now time for me to serve him. Then, serve with love and a smile.

How will I be remembered?

Remind the person of the good things he has done—his work, his family, coaching his children's softball games, caring for his dying parents, and all the good things he has done. The words I used with my husband is that we were a good team, good partners. I used these words to remind him that in a team everyone has a job. We split duties. What I was now doing as a caregiver was part of being on the team. I said it often and he would respond that we were a good team!

As a chaplain, it has been my experience that the dying often experience a feeling of acceptance as they come near death. A friend whom I dearly loved fought death to almost the end. Then, as I was leaving at the end of a visit very near the end of her life, she said, "I don't know why I feel such peace, but I do." I was extremely comforted to know that she had found peace.

Signs and Symptoms of Approaching Death

This information comes directly from the Hospice of Midland handbook. These are important things for the caregiver and family to know so I have included them verbatim:

"The Hospice staff realize that this particular period is one of the most difficult times you and your family will have to live through. Our approach in all matters affecting you during this time is to be as honest and straightforward as possible. In this way, the Hospice team members can establish a trusting and open communications relationship with your family member who is very ill and the members of your family who are concerned about the possibility of approaching death. Your Hospice nurse, volunteer, and physician are your best resources to help you clarify your concerns about this information. NOT ALL THESE SYMPTOMS WILL APPEAR AT THE SAME TIME AND MAY NEVER APPEAR. We want to relate each possible symptom to you in order to decrease your fear if one should appear suddenly. All the symptoms described are indicative of how the body prepares itself for the final stage of life."

1. The arms and legs of the body may become cool to the touch and you may notice the underside of the body becoming much darker in color. These symptoms are a result of blood circulation slowing down.

2. The Hospice patient will gradually spend more and more time sleeping during the day and at all times will be difficult to arouse. This symptom is a result of a change in the body's metabolism.

3. Your family member may become increasingly confused about time, place, and identity of close and familiar people. Again, this is a result of body metabolism changes.

4. Incontinence (loss of control) of urine and bowel movements is often not a problem until death becomes imminent.

5. Oral secretions may become profuse and collect in the back of the throat. You may have heard friends refer to a "death rattle". This symptom is a result in a decrease in the body's intake of fluids and inability to cough up normal saliva production.

6. Clarity of hearing and vision decreases slightly.

7. You may notice your loved one becoming restless, pulling at bed linen, and having visions of people or things which do not exist. These symptoms are a result of a decrease in the oxygen circulation to the brain and a change in the body's metabolism.

8. Your family member will decrease need for food and drink because the body will naturally begin to conserve energy which is expended on these tasks.

9. During sleep, at first, you will notice breathing patterns in your loved one change to an irregular place where there may be 10-30 second periods of not breathing. Your doctor and nurse refer to this as "apnea". This symptom is very common and indicative of a decrease in circulation and build up on body waste products.

10. If your loved one has a bladder catheter in place, you will notice that the amount of urine will decrease as death comes close.

11. Keep warm blankets, but not electric, on the bed to keep him from being cold.

12. Plan your times for visitors for those times when he/she seems most alert.

13. Remind your family member frequently: what day it is, what time it is, and who is in the room and talking to them.

14. Place pads under the incontinent patient and use other hygiene techniques for cleanliness.

15. Provide a cool mist humidifier to increase the humidity in the room when oral secretion builds up. Elevating the head with pillow or obtaining a hospital bed will make breathing easier. Ice chips, a straw, and cool, moist wash cloths will relieve feelings of dehydration.

16. Keep lights on in the room when vision decreases and never assume the patient cannot hear you. Hearing is the last of the senses to be lost.

17. Talk calmly and assuredly with the confused person so as not to startle or frighten them further.

18. Refer to a nutrition sheet for good information and supplements.

19. Elevating the head of the bed often relieves the person who has irregular breathing patterns.
20. Consult with a nurse as the urine output decreases, for there is a possible need to irrigate the catheter to prevent blockage.

Advance
Directives

Everyone should discuss advanced care, make decisions, and document those decisions with family members, physicians, and maybe even attorneys. Even if you are not sick now, planning for health care in the future is an important step. Do it now before you are either too ill or incapacitated by an accident. If you are unable to speak for yourself, these directives can speak for you.

What are some of the decisions that could come up?

- Cardiopulmonary resuscitation
- Use of a ventilator

- Feeding tubes
- Comfort care. Comfort care includes managing shortness of breath; limiting medical testing; spiritual and emotional counseling; and giving pain medications for pain, anxiety, nausea, or constipation.

An advance directive can state clearly whether staying alive as long as possible is your desire or state when you would no longer want to have life prolonged. These are things that can change with age or with changes in your health. An advance directive can be changed as you age or as your health changes. It can be very important to have these wishes written well in advance of a stroke, an accident, or even Alzheimer's disease or dementia begins, and the patient can no longer express their wishes. And, it is much easier for the caregiver if these wishes and very difficult decisions are made in a time not as stressful as when the actual need presents itself.

These directives can include, but are not limited to, a living will and a durable power of attorney for health care.

A living will is a written document that helps you tell doctors how you want to be treated if you are dying or permanently unconscious and cannot make your own decisions about emergency treatment. In a living will, you can say which of the procedures described above you want, which ones you don't want, and under what conditions each of your choices apply.

A durable power of attorney for health care is a legal document naming a health care proxy, someone to make medical decisions for you at a time when you are unable to do so. Your proxy, also known as a representative, surrogate, or agent, should be familiar with your values and wishes. This means that he or she will be able to decide as you would when treatment decisions need to be made. Having a health care proxy helps you plan for situations that cannot be foreseen, like a serious auto accident. The proxy can evaluate each situation or treatment option independently if that is your desire.

Other advance care planning documents could include:

- Do not resuscitate orders
- Organ and tissue donations

You may want to go online and print out an advance directive card for your wallet. This will notify health care workers about your decisions. The caregiver or responsible member of the family, you will need to gather, catalog, and place documents in a safe place. This list is a good place to begin, but if you begin the process at the beginning of caregiving, you will hopefully have enough time to complete the process. (Also, the sooner you begin, the greater the likelihood that the patient can assist you!)

- Birth certificate
- Driver's license
- Social Security card
- Medicare card
- Insurance card
- Mortgage records
- Any titles to autos, boats, motorcycles
- Power of attorney
- Marriage certificate
- Divorce certificate
- Military records
- Living will, health care proxy, advance directives
- Durable power of attorney
- Trust instruments
- Wills
- Long-term care insurance information
- Personal health records
- Credit cards

Just the Facts

IMPORTANT TELEPHONE NUMBERS	
Family	

Friends	
Neighbors	

Pharmacy	
Physician	
Medical equipment (oxygen, rented hospital beds, wheelchairs, etc.)	
Accountant/financial consultant	
Attorney	
Clergy	
Insurance Agent	
Bank Officer	
Stockbroker	
Handyman	
Plumber	
Electrician	
Car maintenance	
Repairs	
Oil change	
Tire store	

Warranties	
Car Registration/ insurance information	
Roofer	
Furrier	
Dentist	
Hearing aid specialist	
Vision specialist	
ALARM SYSTEM	
Telephone #	
Alarm code to dismiss alarm	
CELL PHONE CARRIER	
User names/ password	
EXTRA KEYS	
House	
Auto	
File Cabinets	

Safe Codes	
BANKS	
Account numbers	
User names/ passwords	
Direct deposit information	
Safe deposit box key	
INVESTMENT ACCOUNTS	
User names/ passwords	
Loans	
• Name of institution	
• Account numbers	
MONTHLY RECURRING EXPENSES	
House payment information	
Utilities	
Insurance	
Mortgage	
Cable	

Cell phones	
Car payment	
HOA fees	
Credit cards	
Loans	
Computer username/ passwords	
PET INFORMATION	
Veterinary	
Type of dog food	
Allergies/ medications	

Again, it is best to complete this list long before you need it and update as things change. After the information is compiled, it can be on a hard copy and on a USB stored in a separate place. One could be stored in a personal fire-proof safe and another in a bank deposit box or online in "the cloud." We do live in a world where information can be stolen and used by others, so it is important to keep the information safe and never left out on a counter or open space.

If the caregiver is not a spouse, it is imperative that the caregiver ask who will be taking care of the mail and daily business of paying bills, etc. If the caregiver is a spouse, he/she should begin to take care of the checkbooks/bill paying. There are too many widows who have never paid a bill. After the death of a spouse is not a time to learn something as stressful as statement reconciling.

This is a great time to speak with an attorney about adding an additional signatory to bank accounts and investment accounts. Check to ascertain what the best thing to do is in the case of a death. Accounts become inaccessible if they are styled "Mr. and Mrs." rather than "Mr. or Mrs." I added my adult son to my accounts soon after the death of my husband. He fought the process. Our children do not want to talk about a parent's possible death. I made it easier by saying for him to think about what it would mean if I were touring Italy and became hospitalized for a broken leg while zip lining. He laughed and we completed the process!

Appendix I

Common Grief Reactions

Sadness
Anxiety
Guilt and regret
Fatigue
Suicidal feelings
Helplessness
Hopelessness

Anger
Shock
Loneliness
Relief
Depression
Numbness

Physical Sensations

Hollowness in stomach   Tightness in the throat

Tightness in the chest

Weakness in the muscles

Digestive problems

Blurred vision

Over-sensitivity to noise

Lack of energy

Headache

Symptoms of the person who died

Behaviors

Sleep disturbance

Dreams of the deceased

Sighing

Inability to concentrate

Lack of strength

Increased use of cigarettes

Alcohol or sedatives[1]

Social withdrawal

Indifference

Absentminded behavior

Bland expression

Lack of energy

Weight loss or gain

Looking for objects that remind the survivor of the deceased

---

1   I would like to caution you to be very careful with any substance that you use to dull your pain whether it be alcohol, sleeping medications, anxiety medications, or any other substance. First, you don't really want to totally dull your senses. That statement may seem antithetical to how you are feeling. However, you want to feel these feelings and work through them, not dull them, and need to do this healing at some point in the future. Death is a terrible hurt that needs to be addressed, walked through, and healed. Talking these feelings out is the best way to face them. Hearing the pain expressed verbally seems to help your brain to work through anger and eventually find acceptance. For myself, I made a rule to never drink alone. I am not much of a drinker anyway, but I knew that I would never become a closet drinker with the rule of never drinking alone!

Changes in Thinking

Disbelief

Sense of presence[2]

Slow thinking
and reactions

Confusion

Hallucinations

Preoccupation and need
to tell and retell details
of recent events

---

2 I have spoken with a great number of people who feel the presence of their loved
   one. One frequent occurrence is waking up at night and feeling their presence in the
   room, almost as if you are being watched over. I've had people relate that they felt
   the moment that their loved one's spirit left their body. The feeling seems to be that
   their loved one stays until he/she feels that their presence is no longer required. It's
   a very sweet feeling.

Appendix II

The Do's and Don'ts of Comforting the Grieving

First, let me say that this is such a difficult subject and a challenge for all of us, especially if you have not had to face death/grieving before. These are guidelines. Be aware that even as I write this, I cringe at the things I have done that I wish to take back! So, I am not passing judgment! I have been guilty of saying/doing some of these things both before and after the death of my husband. When we are attempting to comfort the grieving, we can easily become flustered or don't take time to think before we speak and some of these things just come out! Do better next time! That is always my goal!

And, remember that just because something is true does not make it helpful.

Don't Say

- They are in a better place.
- You will see him again (for Christians).
- It's time to go on with your life.
- Please don't talk about him—it makes me sad.
- Give it time.
- Keep busy.
- Be strong
- At least he didn't suffer. /At least he's no longer suffering.
- He lived a long life.
- Try not to think about it.
- You'll be stronger because of this.
- Be glad you had him for as long as you did.
- He wouldn't have wanted to live like this.
- He wouldn't want you to be sad.
- Life is for the living.
- Have you considered counseling?
- It's time to move on.
- You can have another child

What Not to Do

- Don't stay away and ignore it because you don't know what to say.

- Don't engage in conversation and not mention the deceased.
- Don't feel bad if the person cries. More than likely they will.
- Don't forget the grieving person after a couple of months; this is when the going gets more difficult.
- Don't interject your own theology.
- Don't make the person feel guilty for not feeling spiritual, friendly, engaging, interested.
- Don't pray without first asking.
- Don't personalize—this is not about you. Don't tell horror stories about your Aunt Jane.
- Don't assail a person in a public place. They may be trying to hold it together to get an errand done.
- Don't compare with statements like, "It's not as hard to lose an aunt as losing a best friend." Their aunt could have been their best friend.
- Do not offer advice.
- Don't judge or criticize either the griever or the deceased.

Helpful Things to Say

- I am so very sorry.
- I can't imagine your loss
- I'm sorry you are going through this.

- I wish it were different.

It is not your job to make the grieving person feel better—you can't anyway! Weep with them! Reach out and touch them. Give them a hug. Touch their hand. The less you say, the less opportunity to say the wrong thing! Just be there!

It has been pointed out to me that this is a short list. Yes, it is extremely brief. The point here is if you stay with few words, it is much more difficult to make a hurtful statement. I'm so sorry you are hurting is probably as helpful as you can get.

Helpful Things to Do

- Write a note or send an email or text. This allows the grieving person to read it at their own time—or again and again if they find it comforting.
- Be there.
- Take food, but don't overwhelm. No one wants to spend the day dealing with too much food.
- Offer to dog-sit.
- Offer to housesit during the funeral services.
- Offer to be a coordinator—for food, for scheduling food, carpool of children's activities.
- Offer to watch the house if they are going out of town—pick up the papers and mail, etc.

- Call when you are going to the grocery store and offer to pick up bread, milk, chocolate, wine.
- Do call before you go by.
- Share your favorite books—one at a time.
- After a period of time, invite the person to attend a special event with you—birthday party, bunco party, dinner with friends, social event, concert.
- Say the name of the deceased often.
- Tell an amusing story about the deceased.
- Listen while they talk about the deceased.
- Carry tissues. Tears will come.
- Give a lot of grace.
- Ask the grieving person to tell their story of loss, even if you know it. It is healing for them to tell the story again and again. (My own personal belief is that this helps to own the death of the loved one too, to leave denial behind and work toward acceptance.)

Resources

On Grief *and Grieving*, Elisabeth Kubler-Ross, Simon & Shuster, 2005

A Grace Disguised, Jerry Sittser, Zondervan, 1995

Option B, Sheryl Sandberg, Knopf, 2017

Yellow Balloons, Tim Dunn, Equip Press, 2018

Servant Leadership, David Kuhnert, AuthorHouse, 2016

Shattered Dreams, Larry Crabb, Waterbrook Press, 2001

Love Does, Bob Goff, Nelson Books, 2012

www.a-zquotes.com, C.S. Lewis

www.brainyquotes.com,W. B. Yeats

desiringgod.org

Griefshare.org

Hospice of Midland Training Material, Kristi Elsom, Marie Hall, Mary Lou Cassidy

It's Ok That You're Not Ok, Megan Devine – FaceBook

All scripture from the New King James Version

Made in the USA
San Bernardino, CA
21 May 2019